The

MERITS *of*
WOMEN

"Do you really believe," Cornelia replied, "that everything historians tell us about men—or about women—is actually true? You ought to consider the fact that these histories have been written by men, who never tell the truth except by accident."

MODERATA FONTE

The
MERITS *of*
WOMEN

Wherein Is Revealed Their NOBILITY

and Their SUPERIORITY

to Men

MODERATA FONTE
(MODESTA POZZO)

Edited, Translated, and Abridged by VIRGINIA COX
With a New Foreword by DACIA MARAINI

THE UNIVERSITY OF CHICAGO PRESS ◆ CHICAGO AND LONDON

The University of Chicago Press, Chicago 60637
The University of Chicago Press, Ltd., London
© 2018 by The University of Chicago
Foreword © 2018 Dacia Maraini
Published 2018
Printed in the United States of America

23 22 21 20 19 18   1 2 3 4 5 6 7 8 9

ISBN-13: 978-0-226-55063-3 (paper)
ISBN-13: 978-0-226-55077-0 (e-book)
DOI: https://doi.org/10.7208/chicago/9780226550770.001.0001

Portions of this text were originally published by The University of Chicago Press
as *The Worth of Women: Wherein Is Clearly Revealed Their Nobility and Their
Superiority to Men*, edited and translated by Virginia Cox, as part of the series The
Other Voice in Early Modern Europe. © 1997 by The University of Chicago.

Library of Congress Cataloging-in-Publication Data

Names: Fonte, Moderata, 1555–1592, author. | Cox, Virginia, translator, editor. |
  Maraini, Dacia, writer of foreword.
Title: The merits of women : wherein is revealed their nobility and their
  superiority to men / Moderata Fonte (Modesta Pozzo) ; edited, translated, and
  abridged by Virginia Cox ; with a new foreword by Dacia Maraini.
Other titles: Merito delle donne. English
Description: Chicago : The University of Chicago Press, 2018. | Includes
  bibliographical references.
Identifiers: LCCN 2017043482 | ISBN 9780226550633 (pbk. : alk. paper) | ISBN
  9780226550770 (e-book)
Subjects: LCSH: Women—Early works to 1800. | Women—Social conditions—
  Early works to 1800. | Women—History—Renaissance, 1450–1600.
Classification: LCC HQ1148.F6513 2018 | DDC 305.4—dc23
LC record available at https://lccn.loc.gov/2017043482

Contents

Publisher's Note

THE UNIVERSITY OF CHICAGO PRESS first published Virginia Cox's translation of Moderata Fonte's *Il merito delle donne* as *The Worth of Women* as part of our Other Voice in Early Modern Europe series; still in print, that version includes scholarly apparatuses such as footnotes, appendices, and other contextualizing material. This abridgment is an experiment in seeking a more general audience for Fonte's witty, elegant, and surprisingly timely treatise. For this edition, Professor Cox has abridged her masterful translation, crafted a new introduction, and translated Dacia Mariani's new foreword from the Italian. We are delighted to reissue this remarkable book at a moment when its message resonates all the more loudly.

Foreword

HOW DIFFERENTLY THE TWO AUTHORS of this book strike us, Modesta Pozzo (the author's real name) and Moderata Fonte (her pseudonym)—and yet we are talking about the same person. As described by her uncle, Giovanni Niccolò Doglioni, who assumed the role of a father toward her until he gave her away in marriage, Modesta comes over as a quiet and retiring creature, devoted to her family and her husband. This despite the fact that her education had been exceptional for a woman of that era, fostering a sense of independence; she was encouraged as a girl to express her literary talent and left free to devote her time to reading and study.

It is curious that Doglioni's contribution to *The Merits of Women*, the last and most important book by the niece he doted on, should consist of a portrait (an admiring one) of a woman and a character so utterly remote from the atmosphere that we breathe as soon as we open the pages of the work—so remote from the person we imagine bent over her own pages, intent on her reading, or on writing her verse. There is nothing in Doglioni's portrait of the bold and challenging author we see right from the first pages of the dialogue—nothing of the true Moderata Fonte.

Moderata, quite contrary to the modest Venetian lady of the biography, shows startling originality and audacity, evident from the way in which she constructs the work. She decides to stage a meeting between seven women, very different among themselves, but all well educated and, above all, close friends, speaking about a subject that interests them all closely—men.

We are in late sixteenth-century Venice, and it is hard to believe that a lady of the city's bourgeoisie should have shown such capacity for intelligence and astuteness, and such extraordinary forcefulness in unmasking the strategies of patriarchal power. Even Veronica Franco, a courtesan of the time and a great poet (and certainly a woman with a better knowledge of the world of men than Fonte)—even Franco, conscious though she was of the vices and abuses of men, did not rebel in this way against the established male power structure. Not even the challenging, sarcastic Veronica went as far to imagine a cool-eyed treatise on men of the kind that Moderata produced.

> "Just you try finding me a man in all the annals and chronicles of ancient times whose merits stretch to the thousandth part of the rare excellencies and divine qualities of our Lady, the Queen of Heaven. I don't think you're going to have much luck there!" (47)

Just as on a stage (ahead of her time in this also, and anticipating a certain eighteenth-century theatrical manner), the author chooses to bring together her seven female friends in a beautiful garden, belonging to one of them, where they gather to talk about these men who are fathers to them, husbands, sons, brothers.

> "We've already done too much keeping quiet in the past," Leonora replied, "and the more we keep quiet, the worse they get. If a man needs to reclaim some money from a person who has refused to pay him and he keeps quiet about it, the unscrupulous debtor will never give him satisfaction." (81)

Arguments of this kind keep coming, with continual references to history, to literature, to poetry, as well as to life experience. We find moments when "poor men" are defended (although it has to be said that never before had "poor men" been exposed in quite this way). "Men do have some merits when they are married—which is to say, when they are united with a wife. Now that I don't deny." (19) But the whole of the first day, out of the two that the seven friends spend together, does not lean far in the direction of softness toward men. There is always someone ready to debunk any attempt at forgiveness or defense.

> "But without help from their wives, men are just like unlit lamps: in themselves, they are no good for anything, but, when lit, they can be handy to have around the house." (19)

These women bring forward examples of remarkable women, deserving of honor and esteem, with stories that are told, perhaps for the first time, because they serve as a warning, as a model of something that should not be repeated. These are tales from the past, told by women who live their whole lives in a state of servitude to a man—tales of heroines who sacrificed themselves for their companions.

> "You haven't mentioned those women in Sparta," said Cornelia, "who, when their husbands were in prison, obtained permission from the enemy to visit their men and then removed their feminine clothes and dressed their men in them, remaining in the prison themselves to be killed as a punishment while they sent their men out of danger." (51)

What is it that impels the seven friends to engage with such a thorny and potentially explosive theme? What gives them the ability and the courage to confront the enemy (the beloved enemy): men? Paradoxically, it is precisely their experience, their awareness, their understanding—taken together, everything they have learned through their study and their absorption of culture. Seven women, with very different life histories, with very different interests, but united in this consuming desire for knowledge, which in itself places them on the same level as the other sex—indeed, in some cases, higher than the men in their lives. The education that male power had denied them for centuries, out of fear of competition, now becomes the subtle, flexible instrument through which women can unmask the injustice and discrimination to which they want to testify through their own voices.

"Maybe we should just try keeping quiet for a while," said Helena, "and perhaps they'll change their tune."

"We've already done too much keeping quiet in the past," Leonora replied, "and the more we keep quiet, the worse they get." (81)

Yet Fonte's discussion of the merits of women is cut through with continual doubts. Is there a risk that, by criticizing men, they will end up as their permanent enemies? The speakers in the dialogue are quite aware that, whatever men's failings, they cannot do without them. Most of them aspire to find some kind of contact, some kind of tacit agreement.

Is this a contradiction? A backward step, by comparison with the previous, more challenging positions? I would say no. At most, we are maybe looking at a different way to exploit women's intelligence: an intelligence that does not provoke fear and hatred, but rather hope and understanding.

"... I haven't been speaking out of any hatred for men, but rather in a spirit of charity, and moved by the compassion I feel for the many suffering women I see around me. For many men see the world in a blinkered way, and are so firmly convinced by the un-warrantable fallacy that they are created women's superiors that they believe themselves fully justified in treating women as tyran-nically and brutally as they like. But if they could be persuaded of their error, they might just change their ways." (95)

Moderata Fonte, in her *The Merits of Women*, strikes us as a mod-ern feminist, and in the structure of the book and its speakers we can catch distant echoes of the consciousness-raising groups in which many of us first began to speak about our own lives, our relationships with men, our dramas, our hopes, without the fear of being judged or condemned, in the name of a female solidarity which, like any uto-pia, may not be valid always and inevitably, but which has certainly transformed our lives.

Dacia Maraini
(translated by Virginia Cox)
July 2017

Introduction

VIRTUALLY UNKNOWN BEFORE THE 1980s, Moderata Fonte's 1592 dialogue *The Merits of Women* has now taken its place among the great classics of early feminist thought, alongside works such as Christine de Pizan's *Book of the City of Ladies*, which precedes it by almost two centuries, and Mary Wollstonecraft's *Vindication of the Rights of Women*, which follows it by the same length of time. Vividly imagined, challenging, witty, *The Merits of Women* is a significant work of literature, as well as a sometimes startlingly original discussion of women's status. It is difficult to think of a work written before the eighteenth century that so powerfully evokes the realities of women's daily lives and thinks so boldly about their "worth" and their due.

LIFE AND CONTEXT Moderata Fonte was born as Modesta Pozzo in Venice in 1555—in English terms, three years before Elizabeth I succeeded to the throne, and nine years before the birth of Shakespeare and Marlowe. Orphaned as an infant, Modesta was brought up first in a convent and then in her grandmother's household, impressing all around by her brilliance as a child. The engaging biography of Fonte written by her one-time guardian Giovanni Niccolò Doglioni (included in this edition) speaks of her as largely self-educated, reading her way through her step-grandfather's library and pestering her brother to teach her

Latin each evening when he returned from school. The family was a moneyed one: not from the governing patrician class of Venice, which gazes out at us scarlet-robed from the portraits of Veronese and Titian, but from the city's other elite class, known as *cittadini originari*—literally, "original citizens"—who staffed the government's administrative offices and the professions.

Fonte wrote from an early age, and, profiting from Doglioni's contacts, she published her first work at the age of twenty-six, in 1581: a romance of chivalry entitled *Floridoro*, telling the adventures of a young knight of that name. It is here that we first see her adopting her pseudonym, Moderata Fonte, which transforms her given name, meaning literally "Modest Well," into the more euphonious and assertive "Moderate Fountain (or Spring)." The pseudonym celebrates Fonte's creativity, playing on the traditional association of poetry with the Castalian Fountain on Parnassus, home to the Muses. At the same time, it leaves behind the bashful quality of "modesty," so often associated with silence and self-effacement in women. Fonte's pseudonym instead proclaims her "moderation": a virtue suggestive of capacities for reason and self-discipline that not all of Fonte's contemporaries acknowledged that women possessed.

In 1583, at the age of twenty-seven—late for the period—Fonte married a young government lawyer named Filippo Zorzi. By 1587, the couple already had three children. The demands of her young family slowed Fonte's literary production, although she did continue to write. In addition to the works she published before her marriage (the *Floridoro*; a philosophical masque; and a verse narrative of Christ's passion), we have two later surviving works by her: a sequel to her passion narrative, recounting Christ's resurrection, and her masterpiece, *The Merits of Women*. From internal references, the composition of *The Merits* may be dated to the period 1588–92. These were Fonte's last years; according to Doglioni's poignant account, she finished the dialogue the night before she died of childbirth at the age of thirty-seven in 1592.

We are accustomed to thinking of premodern women writers as beleaguered figures, who struggled to assert themselves within a society that conceived narrowly of women's abilities and role. This is clearly true to some extent of Moderata Fonte. Doglioni tells us that she was was forced to dash off her literary works in the moments she could spare from her domestic duties, in deference to the "false notion" that "women should excel at nothing other than the running of their household." The fact that Doglioni brands this notion "false," however, alerts us to the fact that such prejudices were not universal in Fonte's culture. Indeed, it seems to be the case that Venice was more conservative in its attitudes to women than nearby cities on the Venetian mainland, such as Verona and Vicenza, let alone nearby court cultures such as Mantua and Ferrara, where aristocratic ladies took a leading cultural role.

Fonte was well aware of this freer culture beyond the bounds of her city. She spent summers as a child on her grandfather's estate near Sacile, in Friuli, north of Venice, and her correspondents included a young female writer of the Venetian mainland, Issicratea Monti of Rovigo, so famed for her eloquence that she was selected while still an adolescent to deliver an oration to a visiting Hapsburg empress. Fonte also seems to have had contacts in Ferrara and to have known, at least by fame, the virtuoso singer Laura Peverara, one of the great female stars of that court.

As these examples suggest, women enjoyed a relatively high degree of cultural visibility in Italy in this period, by comparison with other countries in Europe. Already in the fifteenth century, we find a scattering of learned Italian women participating in the movement we now know as Renaissance humanism, based around the study and imitation of classical Greek and Roman culture. In the sixteenth century, as the vernacular rose to rival Latin as a literary language, and as literacy spread with the advance of print technology, women began to write in more significant numbers and to see their work published. The 1540s and 1550s saw a cluster of outstanding female poets active in Italy, including the Venice-based Gaspara Stampa, author of some of the most vivid and striking love lyrics of the Italian Renaissance, and the Roman Vittoria Colonna, a powerful innovator within the tradition of Italian religious verse.

Moderata Fonte was, therefore, not breaking new ground as a woman in aspiring to write and publish. This should not, however, lead us to underestimate the boldness and novelty of her work. Down to the mid sixteenth century, women's writing had been largely limited to the genres of lyric poetry and letter-writing. When Fonte launched her literary career in her mid-twenties by publishing a lengthy chivalric romance, it was a highly unusual gesture, setting down a new marker for Italian women's literary ambition. The same may be said of *The Merits of Women*. While it is not the first work in dialogue form to have been written by a woman, its scale, its complex architecture, and its broad thematic range mark it out as something quite new. Not since the days of Christine de Pizan, in the early fifteenth century, had a woman attempted writings of this scale and ambition; but, where de Pizan was an outlier, Fonte anticipated a strong trend in women's writing in Italy. Between 1580 and 1620, Italian women published over sixty single-authored works, including epics, pastoral dramas, a tragedy, and prose and verse narratives of many kinds.

**DIALOGUE AND DEBATE
IN *THE MERITS OF WOMEN***

Like many popular literary forms of the Italian Renaissance, the dialogue form was a classical borrowing, shaped by the influence of ancient writers such as Plato, Cicero, and Lucian. At their most basic, dialogues could be dry Q&As between stickperson speakers in a thinly realized setting. At their most elaborate, they could be richly imaginative works of art, offering vivid speech portraits of particular social microcultures, while at the same time canvassing cultural and philosophical questions in a sophisticated and entertaining way. The play of contrasting opinion is the animating force of the genre. One sixteenth-century theorist compared the dialogue to an intellectual tinderbox, striking sparks of truth through the clash of ideas. In modern terms, we might speak of the dialogue form "gamifying" the processes of knowledge production and transmission. Dialogues frequently organize their represented conversation as a competitive debating game. This is the model we see in *The Merits of Women*, where one group of interlocutors is given the role of speaking ill of men, the other of taking up their defense.

Few sixteenth-century writers of dialogue handle the form with such aplomb and vivacity as Moderata Fonte. She makes the unusual choice to write a dialogue with a group of women as the sole interlocutors, engaged in what the work defines as a "domestic conversation"—informal, affectionate, spontaneous. At various points, the speakers comment on the freedom they feel, conversing without the constraining presence of men. Many sixteenth-century dialogues descend into effective monologues, with one speaker dominating the discussion, but Fonte is careful to keep the dialogue more freeflowing. The learned young poet Corinna, whom some critics have seen as Fonte's alter ego, is the closest the dialogue comes to a dominant speaker; but even Corinna is rarely allowed a speech of more than a page without one of her companions jumping in to contradict her, or to take the conversation in a new path.

Fonte gives shape to her dialogue by the debate structure mentioned earlier, and the "pro- and anti-men" theme, which runs through the whole work. She balances structure, however, with a feel for the drift of a natural conversation, showing the speakers frequently wandering off-path. This is especially so on the second day of the dialogue, where, at the urging of her companions, Corinna engages in a series of "scientific" disquisitions, on the natural world (animals, fish, plants, stones, rivers, and springs) and on the social and cultural world (the Venetian government and the professions and arts), clearly intended to give the dialogue a more encyclopedic scope. Corinna's digressions are constantly interrupted by the exasperated hostess, Leonora, who attempts to bring the dialogue back round to its agreed anti-men theme.

Fonte uses this device of Leonora's repeated frustrations with considerable subtlety, as a means of calling attention to the deeper thematic unity that underlies the dialogue's apparent digressiveness. Corinna's learned speeches on the natural world, though apparently off-topic, connect profoundly with the feminist themes of the dialogue. Women will only find a way to escape their position of subjection by means of education, and by taking symbolic and discursive possession of the world that surrounds them. The second book of *The*

Merits takes women outside the walls of the household and makes the whole universe their domain.

NATURE, CUSTOM, AND THE HIERARCHY OF THE SEXES

The natural world, as portrayed in the second book of *The Merits of Women*, is a purposive one, and essentially benign, despite mentions of earthquakes, famines, and poisons. God has created the great mechanism of the world as a habitat for humankind, his most beloved creation. Divine Providence has secreted healing powers into plants, spa waters, and precious stones to help us preserve our health, and it has filled the world with fruits and crops and animals for our nourishment and pleasure. One of the most lyrical passages in the second book hymns "friendship" (*amicizia*) as the governing principle of the universe, bonding the elements in harmony at a cosmic level, just as it bonds individuals and communities in peace and love.

It is against this background of natural harmony and cosmic "friendship" that the feminist speakers of *The Merits of Women* set the distinctly unfriendly social relationship between the sexes in the Venice of their day. Men and women are of the same species, the same flesh and blood, and they were created by God as companions for one another; yet men have so convinced themselves of their superiority to women that they have lost sight of this fundamental truth. Women are "otherized"; considered as lesser beings; deprived of the resources and education that might allow them to maintain themselves; forced into a position of humiliating dependence in which they must accept whatever harsh treatment their husbands or fathers choose to inflict. They are victims of "tyranny," of illegitimate rule—an accusation of special potency in Venice, which prided itself as a rare beacon of republican liberty in a Europe mainly governed by monarchical regimes.

The notion that men's rule over women constituted a tyranny was a challenging idea for the period, at a philosophical level, as well as that of social critique. The philosophical orthodoxy of the day, deriving from the ancient Greek thinker Aristotle, saw women's subjection to men as a legitimate part of the natural order, not as an abuse or perversion. Indeed, Aristotle took the structure of the household as a paradigm for political organization, precisely on account of its supposed naturalness. Free adult males were dominant by right within the household, as the most rational and perfect exemplars of the human species. Women, children, and slaves were variously subordinate, precisely because their weaker rationality fitted them to obey, not to rule.

Fonte was not the first thinker to challenge this orthodoxy. On the contrary, a body of argument had grown up in the fifteenth and sixteenth centuries arguing against Aristotle's hierarchical view of the sexes, and sustaining the alternative view that women were men's equals by nature and that their subordination was a matter of custom. With the exception of Christine de Pizan, however, most writers who had argued for this position down to the late sixteenth century were men, often writing in a detached, theoretical manner, to the extent that some scholars have considered the Renaissance *querelle des femmes* ("debate on women") as little more than an intellectual game or an opportunity for rhetorical display.

The Merits of Women is very different. Fonte does incorporate standard features of Renaissance "defenses of women," such as a list of famous women of classical antiquity, and a learned discussion of physiology, and the humoral make-up of men's and women's bodies (cold and humid, according to medical tradition, in the case of women; hot and dry in the case of men). These more conventional and learned elements make up a relatively small part of her feminist speakers' arguments, however; for the most part, they rely on experience and observation, describing the predicament of women in contemporary Venetian society in an unprecedentedly circumstantial and impassioned way. It is part of the power of the dialogue, as well as its charm, that it embeds its arguments within such a vividly realized social context. Fonte is concerned with proving women's worth at a theoretical level, but she is far more concerned with what recognition of this worth on the part of society would mean concretely for women's lives.

THE SINGLE SELF　　Fonte's boldest experiment in this speculative vein is to imagine an alternative Venice in which women might decide freely to opt out of marriage: the defining life experience in this period for women in this period, with the exception of nuns. The best-educated woman in *The Merits of Women*, Corinna, speaks trenchantly of her decision to remain single, while her feminist companion-in-arms Leonora, a young widow, pronounces that she would rather drown than marry again. The setting of the dialogue is a garden designed by an aunt of Leonora's who made the same life choice as Corinna, featuring as its centerpiece an allegorical fountain that serves as a manifesto for the joys of a freely chosen single life.

How much this choice of singledom was a reality for Venetian women at the time is an interesting question. Fonte intriguingly alludes to Corinna as a "young *dimmessa*," suggesting that she is a member of a tertiary religious order for unmarried laywomen, the

Dimesse, similar to the medieval Flemish beguines. It is possible that a few brave Venetian women did use the Dimessa identity to experiment with life outside marriage in this period, out of choice, rather than because they lacked the financial resources for a dowry. It is equally possible, however, that, in crafting her ideal of heroic singledom, Fonte is translating classical archetypes of female autonomy, such as the Amazons or Diana's huntswomen-nymphs, into modern Venetian terms. Fonte is careful to set her dialogue in a place apart from the real world of Venice—or, better, in a liminal or threshold place, the temporary feminine utopia of Leonora's aunt's garden, suspended somewhere between the fantastic and the real.

Whatever its relationship to historical reality, one function of the advocacy of singledom within *The Merits of Women* is to make a powerful statement about women's capacity for autonomy and yearning for freedom. Freedom is a leitmotif of the dialogue, along with *amicizia*, invoked by Fonte's speakers at each turn. This is highly significant in context. Venice's association with liberty is emphasized from the work's opening lines, where we learn that the sea-borne city is "free as the sea itself," and that her inhabitants enjoy "remarkable freedom." As we see in the course of the dialogue, however, this legendary republican liberty is limited to men, the strutting lords of the city. By contrast, Venice's women lead shackled lives, trapped in their gilded or less gilded cages.

Fonte's exploration of what freedom might look like for women is perhaps the greatest philosophical novelty of *The Merits of Women*. It was axiomatic in Fonte's society that elite women's freedom of movement and interaction must be severely restricted, in order to preserve their sexual "honor" and hence the honor of their families. In this context, juxtaposing the notions of women and freedom could look suspiciously like a recipe for sexual license.

Fonte's feminist speakers scorn the logic of this infantilizing treatment of women, which at its worst can lead them to being "shut up like animals within four walls" (58). Instead, they underline that women are rational beings, capable of regulating themselves morally without the need for external constraint. They also insist that, despite the innate kindness that makes women so crucial to the happiness of the human community, their purpose on earth is not limited to the role of caring for their husbands and children. Fonte's women delight in one another's company; they find pleasure in learning, intellectual engagement, creativity; they relish the freedom to speak unconstrainedly, and to define themselves for themselves. Archaic though aspects of the dialogue are (we no longer believe in the existence of the phoenix, or that the sun moves round the earth), in these respects Fonte's speakers can seem startlingly modern. We may not always recognize our lives in their reality, but we recognize ourselves in their dreams.

Virginia Cox
July 2017

VERA MODERATÆ FONTIS EFFIGIES
ÆTATIS SVÆ ANNO XXXIII.

Portrait of Moderata Fonte from the 1600 edition of *Il merito delle donne*, printed by Domenico Imberti in Florence. The Latin caption reads: "Faithful image of Moderata Fonte in the thirty-fourth year of her life."

Life of Moderata Fonte

The Life, *written in 1593, starts with a description of the marriage of Fonte's parents, Girolamo da Pozzo and Marietta dal Moro. Girolamo was a wealthy young lawyer from the* cittadino *class of Venice (see the introduction), while Marietta was the stepdaughter of another lawyer, Prospero Saraceni. They married in the early 1550s.*

GIROLAMO'S WIFE GAVE HIM THEIR FIRST CHILD, a son named Leonardo, in 1553. Two years later, on the day of Saints Vitus and Modestus, the girl who is the subject of this biography was born, and at her christening in the parish church of San Samuele, she was given the name Modesta. But before Modesta was a year old, both her parents died, and the poor little orphans were left in a state it is only too easy to imagine. The only good thing that can be said was that their relatives fell over one another to take the orphans into their care—along with their inheritance, which gave them an income of five hundred or more ducats a year. The children were placed in the care of their maternal grandmother [Cecilia de' Mazzi] and her husband, Messer Prospero Saraceni, who were diligently seeing to their care and upbringing when suddenly another relative kidnapped the little girl and paid for her to be placed in the convent of Santa Marta.

In the convent, Modesta's lively intelligence proved so engaging that she was showered with love and caresses from all the reverend sisters. The nuns taught her the kind of little recital pieces they usually teach in such places; and her memory proved so keen that no sooner had she read these things once than she could repeat them from memory, to the astonishment of all around. So, whenever some lady came to visit the convent, she would always be taken to see the little girl and hear her perform, as if she were some strange and remarkable freak of nature. One day the convent received a visit from Padre [Gabriele] Fiamma, the famous preacher, and, having listened to the child, he was so astonished that he was moved to say that she truly seemed to him like a pure disembodied spirit, "a spirit without a body." At this, little Modesta turned to the cleric, a great whale of a man, and (thinking, perhaps, that his words were some kind of insult) retorted as quick as a flash that if she seemed to him a spirit without a body, he seemed to her a body without a spirit. The reverend father was very much struck by the speed of the little girl's riposte and the charming manner in which she proffered it.

When Modesta reached the age of nine, she left the convent and returned to Saraceni's house, where she had as a companion a daughter of the latter [Saracena Saraceni], slightly older than herself. And as Saraceni was fond of literature, and especially of poetry, the little girl, to imitate and vie with him, set herself to writing verse herself, as though it was the most natural thing in the world. She succeeded astonishingly well for a child of her age; and Saraceni, recognizing this natural talent on her part, set about stimulating her gift for poetry by constantly suggesting new subjects for her to write about and keeping her supplied with books to read and study. At the same time (amazing to recount), when her brother came home from school, little Modesta would come up and pester him to explain to her what he had been taught that day; and she would so fervently impress what he said on her memory that she retained a great deal more of what he had learned than he himself did. And she so threw herself into the study of letters that she could soon read any Latin book very fluently and could even write fairly well in Latin.

As a child, Modesta devoted herself to writing, with extraordinary results. But it was not simply in writing that she excelled, but in everything she tried. Without any training, she could draw from life any figure placed in front of her, in a way that astounded everyone who saw her. She played the harpsichord and the lute; she sang; her arithmetic was impressive; and her handwriting was clear, swift, and accurate. She was also a superb needlewoman, and without any kind of pattern or sketch to guide her, she could embroider any subject or design that was suggested to her, bringing it to life with her needle before the eyes of the amazed lookers-on.

When Modesta had grown up, I married Saraceni's daughter, who had been her companion. And since the girls had grown up like sisters and she could not bear to be parted from my wife, she came to live with us when we were married and stayed on in our house. Up to this point, her talent had been lying buried; but I immediately recognized it and determined, as a lover of excellence, to reveal it to the world. So I encouraged her writing and started arranging for the publication of her works. During her stay in my household, she wrote the *Floridoro* (not just the cantos that appeared in the published edition, but also others). She also wrote the *Passion of Christ* and countless sonnets, canzoni, and madrigals on different subjects, as well as some masques that were performed before successive doges of Venice.

And so Modesta remained in my house until I decided it was time to arrange a marriage for her; and when someone proposed that distinguished gentleman Messer Filippo de' Zorzi, tax lawyer to the Waterways Office, I gave her to him as a wife, after making all the usual inquiries. There are four surviving children of the marriage, two boys and two girls: the eldest is a boy of ten, followed by a girl of eight and a boy of six. Madonna Modesta brought them up with all possible diligence, perfecting the most refined of skills in them; and certainly, few children of their age can be compared with them, for all the three eldest are already competent in Latin and can sing, sight-read, and play the viola, each playing his or her own part, to the amazement of all around. But (cruel and bitter fate!) as Madonna Modesta gave birth to another little girl—the fourth surviving child—she was suddenly taken ill and died: a great loss for all those she left behind, but especially for her children, poor mites, who have now been deprived of the schooling she alone could have given them (for their father's time is completely taken up by his work).

And so, as I said, Madonna Modesta died in the morning of All Souls' Day of the year 1592. Her death left all those who had known her devastated, with a sorrow from which few of us will ever recover. One remarkable thing is that the very day before she died, she completed a dialogue she had been working on, which she entitled *The Merits of Women:* the very work that is being published alongside this account of her life.

Madonna Modesta was extremely good at running her household: so good, indeed, that her husband scarcely needed to give it a thought. She had such an amazing memory that I have seen her repeat a sermon word for word when she returned home after church. She read amazingly fast, retaining so much of what she was reading that she could give a meticulous summary of the whole. She often used her intelligence to predict exactly what was going to happen, so that it seemed almost as though she were endowed with some divine spirit of prophecy. She wrote poetry so quickly that it seemed almost incredible. One time, Madonna Modesta dreamed up a subject for a poem one evening and the next morning woke up and wrote down thirty-six stanzas she had mentally composed. The *Floridoro*, too, and all her other things, she wrote in the same manner, for, as a woman, she had to attend to womanly tasks like sewing, and she did not wish to neglect these labors because of the false notion, so widespread in our city today, that women should excel in nothing but the running of the household.

When she died, her husband managed to find a burial place for her in the cloister of the Franciscans near San Rocco. There she was buried, and a Latin epitaph can be seen carved in the wall, which reads as follows:

> Here lies Modesta da Pozzo, a most learned woman, who, having felicitously given birth to many offspring of the intellect under the name of Moderata Fonte, both in Tuscan verse and in prose, while engaged in the labors of natural childbirth, gave life to a little girl, but at the same time (alas!) death to herself. Filippo Zorzi, advocate for the Officio dell'Acque, raised this stone to his most beloved wife.

May God, in his infinite goodness, just as in this life he endowed her with intelligence and virtue beyond the normal lot of mankind, deign now in the next life to favor her and admit her among the circle of those most devoted to Him, so that she may enjoy in reality what she most faithfully believed here on earth and most heroically taught in her poetry.

Giovanni Niccolò Doglioni
1593

The
MERITS *of*
WOMEN

"And when it's said that women must be subject to men, the phrase should be understood in the same sense as when we say that we are subject to natural disasters, diseases, and all the other accidents of this life."

First Day

THE MOST NOBLE CITY OF VENICE lies wondrously situated on the farthest shores of the Adriatic Sea; and not only is this city founded on the sea, but the walls that surround her, the fortresses that guard her, and the gates that enclose her are nothing other than that same sea. The sea, divided up and channeled into canals between the houses, forms a convenient thoroughfare, whereby people are ferried from one place to another with the aid of little boats. The sea is the high road of the city and the open countryside around it, through which pass all the goods and traffics that arrive there from various parts.

So this city is utterly different from all others and a novel and miraculous example of God's handiwork. Venice exceeds all other ancient and modern cities in nobility and dignity, so that it may in all justice be called the Metropolis of the universe. Its pomp and glory are beyond calculation; its riches are inexhaustible; and the splendor of the buildings, the sumptuousness of the clothes, the remarkable freedom enjoyed by its inhabitants are things that cannot be imagined or described. It is quite remarkable how everyone loves living there, for it seems as though all newcomers, as soon as they have tasted the sweetness of life there, find it impossible to leave. And this means that there are people of every nationality in the city, and, just as the limbs and arteries of our body are all connected to the heart, so all cities and all parts of the world are connected to Venice. Money flows here as nowhere else and ours is a city as free as the sea itself. And what is most marvelous of all is that although the city harbors such a great diversity of races and customs, nonetheless an incredible peace and justice reign there.

Well then, in this truly divine city, there was once not long ago a group of noble and spirited women, all from the most respected families of the city, who, despite their great differences in age and marital status, were so united by breeding and taste that a tender bond of friendship had formed between them. These women would often steal time together for a quiet conversation; and on these occasions, safe from any fear of being spied on by men or constrained by their presence, they would speak freely on whatever subject they pleased. Sometimes one of them, who was fond of music, taking up her lute or tempering her sweet voice with the notes of a harpsichord, would provide a charming entertainment; or another, whose tastes inclined to poetry, would recite some novel and elegant composition to entertain that judicious audience in a fresh and pleasing manner.

The women were seven in number. The first was Adriana, an elderly widow; the second, a young daughter of hers, of marriageable age, called Virginia; the third, a young widow called Leonora; the fourth, an older married woman called Lucretia. The fifth woman, Cornelia, was a young married woman; the sixth, Corinna, a young *dimmessa*. The seventh, Helena, a young bride, had temporarily left the group, for she had gone to stay with her new husband in a nearby villa on the mainland, and since the wedding none of the others had seen her.

Now this most worthy group of friends, hearing that the young widow Leonora had recently inherited a house with a very lovely garden, decided to pay her a visit there at the first opportunity. And so one day they went in a party to pay a visit on this charming young hostess; and after the usual greetings had passed between them, they repaired at her invitation to a light and airy room (for it was the height of summer). There some—the older ones—went out onto a balcony overlooking the Grand Canal, and lingered there for a while enjoying the fresh air and watching the gondolas flying past below. The others, led by Virginia, drew up to a window that overlooked the garden and stood there larking about as young girls do when they are together, affectionately teasing one another.

After a while, a gondola was seen pulling up to the quay; and, as the women looked at it, wondering whose it could be, they suddenly realized that it belonged to Helena. The young bride had just returned from the country and, hearing that all her friends were assembled at Leonora's, she had come there at once to see them all, and in particular Virginia, who before her marriage had been her closest friend. When the women saw it was Helena arriving, their happiness was complete, for she was a very charming young woman; and she had hardly got up the stairs before they all flocked around her, embracing her and smothering her with kisses. Then they led her into the drawing room, where they all sat down and feasted their eyes upon her; until finally Virginia spoke up and asked her how she had been all this time and whether she was happy.

Before Helena could reply, Leonora, who had a keen wit, cut in with these words: "My dear Virginia, how can you ask such a thing, when everyone already knows the answer? For popular opinion dictates that no new bride can be anything other than happy."

"Well, let's not say happy," added Lucretia. "Rather, as well as can be expected."

"When I think about it," said Helena, "I'm not sure I can say yet whether I'm happy or not. I greatly enjoy my husband's company, but there is one thing about him that dismays me a little. He is quite insistent that I should not leave the house, whereas I long for nothing more than to go to all the weddings and banquets to which I am invited—partly because this is my time for diversion, but also because I'm concerned to keep up my own and my husband's reputation by letting the world see that he is treating me well and that I can dress as befits a gentlewoman, as you can see."

"I hope to God," Cornelia interjected, "that you'll never have anything worse to complain of! But you have yet to learn how quickly a wedding cake can go stale."

"Our 'young married,'" said Lucretia, "is still unconvinced of this truth; she can't make up her mind to believe it. And she's quite right, of course, for everything is lovely when it has the charm of novelty."

"What you mean is that everything *seems* lovely when it has the charm of novelty," said Leonora.

"As to that," replied Lucretia, "seeming good in such cases is much the same as being good. For if something I eat, for example, seems good to my palate, even if it isn't, it's as good as if it were."

"Don't make me laugh," rejoined Leonora. "If that's the case, then we shouldn't wonder at the bakerwoman who, after toiling all day over her hot oven, ran outside to strip off her little ones' clothes, in the belief that they too must be suffering from the heat, without considering that it was the depths of winter!"

Cornelia laughed at Leonora's joke and exclaimed, "Praise God that we are free to do just as we please, even tell jokes like that to make each other laugh, with no one here to criticize us or put us down."

"Exactly," said Leonora. "If a man could hear us now, laughing together like this, how he would scoff! There'd be no end to it!"

"To tell the truth," said Lucretia, "we are only ever really happy when we are alone with other women; and the best thing that can happen to any woman is to be able to live alone, without the company of men."

"Indeed," said Leonora. "For my part, I derive the greatest happiness from living in peace, without a man. For we all know what a marvelous thing freedom is."

"But surely men can't all be bad?" Helena said.

"Would that they weren't!" replied Cornelia. "And please God that you won't soon be in a position to bear witness to it from your own experience!"

"Who knows?" said Virginia. "What if Helena turns out to be lucky?"

"Well, she just might," said Lucretia. "Don't let's lose all hope."

"However badly you speak of men," Helena rejoined, "I don't believe that you will put Virginia off trying out what it's like to have a husband."

"If it were up to me," said Virginia, "I'd prefer to do without one. But I have to obey the wishes of my family."

"When it comes to that, dear child," said Adriana, "I'd be quite happy to respect your opinion, but your uncles have decided you must marry, because you've inherited such a fortune and it needs to be in safe hands, so I really don't know what else I can do with you. But, anyway, keep your spirits up and don't be afraid. Not all men can be the same, and perhaps you may have better luck than the rest."

"Oh, that really is quite a lifeline you're holding out!" cried Leonora. 'That kind of vain hope, which so rarely comes true, has been the ruin of many a poor girl."

"Our boundless hopes often lure us to destruction," said Corinna. "But this vain hope you're talking about doesn't fool me. I'd rather die than submit to a man! My life here with you is too precious for that, safe from the fear of any great rough man trying to rule my life."

"O happy Corinna!" cried Lucretia. "What other woman in the world can compare her lot with yours? Not one! Not a widow, for she cannot boast of enjoying her freedom without having suffered first; not a wife, for she is still in the midst of her suffering; not a young girl awaiting betrothal, for she is waiting for nothing but ill (as the proverb says, 'husbands and hard times are never long in arriving'). Happy, thrice-happy Corinna, and all that follow your example! All the more so since God has endowed you with such a soaring intelligence that you delight in the pursuit of excellence, and devote your every lofty thought to the study of letters, human and divine, so that one might say that you have already embarked on a celestial life while still surrounded by the trials and dangers of this world. Though such trials barely touch you; for, by rejecting all contact with those falsest of creatures, men, you have escaped the tribulations of this world and are free to devote yourself to those glorious pursuits that will win you immortality. But perhaps you should devote that sublime intelligence of yours to writing a volume on this subject, as an affectionate warning to all those poor simple girls who don't know the difference between good and evil, to show them where their true interests lie; for in this way you would become doubly glorious, fulfilling your duties to God and to the world."

"It certainly would be a worthwhile thing to do," said Corinna, "and I must thank you for bringing it to my notice; perhaps one day I shall indeed write such a work."

"But in the meantime, surely you must already have written something on the theme: some sonnet, perhaps?" suggested Adriana.

"Well, yes," she replied, "but not, I fear, with much success."

"Oh come!" exclaimed Adriana. "Give us a little something! It would give us all such pleasure."

At this, all the others gathered around Corinna and pleaded with her so earnestly that finally, to appease them, she recited the following sonnet, with a pleasing air of modesty:

The heart that dwells within my breast is free:
I serve no one, and am no one's but mine own.

Modesty and courtesy are my lifeblood;
Virtue exalts me and chastity adorns me.
My soul yields to God alone, turning back to Him,
Even while still enveloped in the mortal veil;
It scorns the wicked deceptions of the world,
That ensnare and ruin more ingenuous minds.
Beauty, youth, pleasures, and pomp
Are nothing to me, but sacrifices to my pure intent,
Offered up by my own free will and not by chance.
Thus in my green years, as in those more mature,
Since men's deceptions cannot obstruct my path,
I await fame and glory, in life and in death.

The judicious ladies were utterly charmed by the sonnet, both on account of its sentiments, which all applauded, and the ease and dignity of its style. So they all heaped praises on Corinna and begged for a copy of the poem; and Virginia, who was particularly struck by it, entreated Corinna to sing it to them, accompanying herself on the harpsichord; which she did, to universal applause, following it with other songs.

Meanwhile, realizing that the sun had retreated behind some little clouds, they all agreed to go down and enjoy the lovely garden for a while; and so they set off gaily, taking each other by the hand and going down the stairs. When they got to the garden, words could not express how utterly charming they found it. For there were rows of little emerald-green espaliered shrubs, in all kinds of different shapes—some in the form of pyramids, others mushroom-shaped or melon-shaped, or some other shape—alternating with carefully pruned and beauti-fully intermingled laurels, chestnuts, box trees, and pomegran-ates, all cut to precisely the same height, without a leaf out of place. There were the loveliest orange trees and lemon trees to be seen, with such sweet-smelling flowers and fruit that they gladdened the heart with their scent as much as they delighted the eyes. I shall not attempt to list the countless lovely and var-ied carved urns filled with citrus trees and the daintiest flowers of all kinds, nor the quantities of slender myrtles and the fresh lawns of tiny herbs, cut into triangles, ovals, squares, and other charming conceits. There were jasmine arbors, labyrinths of bright ivy, and little groves of shaped box trees that would have astounded any connoisseur. And the fruit! I shall not attempt to describe it, for there were vast quantities of fruits of all kinds, according to the season; and the useful plants, mingled charmingly with the purely decorative, made up such a lovely sight that the women could not rest from exploring.

And in this way, wandering on from one place to the next, they came upon a lovely fountain which stood in the middle of the garden, constructed with indescribably rare and meticu-lous workmanship. All around this fountain, at each of its sides, there stood the statue of a very beautiful woman with braided hair, from whose breasts, as from a double fountain, there art-fully flowed streams of clear, fresh, sweet water. Each of these statues wore a garland of laurel on her head and carried a slen-der olive branch in her left hand, with a little scroll with writ-ing on it wrapped around the branch; while, in her right hand, each carried a different emblem. So that one of them was holding a little snow-white ermine over her shoulder, holding it away from her breast to keep it dry; and the scroll she held in her left hand bore the following verse:

Let this body rather perish than suffer any stain.

The next carried in her right hand an image of the phoenix, who lives unique in the world; and in her left hand she bore the message:

Alone I live for all time; I die and am reborn.

The third carried a sun and her motto read:

Alone and unique, I illuminate myself and all around.

The next was holding a lantern, in whose flame a little butterfly could be seen burning to death; and her scroll bore the words:

Victim of a vision of beauty, I burn through my own doing.

The fifth had as her device a peach, with a leaf from a peach tree and a verse that read:

All too different is the message of the heart from that of the tongue.

But the sixth carried a crocodile and her scroll read:

I first kill my victims and then, when they are dead, mourn them.

The statues as a whole were so precisely carved and so divinely turned that they seemed rather a natural, living thing than something artificial and a product of human skill. And as the women gazed on and marveled at now this thing, now that, in the lovely garden, filled with rapture and wonder, Adriana said to Leonora, "Come, Leonora, what paradise is this? Who could fail to be charmed by this place?"

"It seems to me," added Cornelia, "that since this is a paradise in which food and drink are also on offer, you may be seeing rather a lot of us here." For in the meantime Leonora's maids had arrived on her orders with the finest wines and sweetmeats as refreshments for the group.

"I am only sorry you have not been before," replied Leonora, "and I hope now you will all wish to return soon."

"I shouldn't make too much of a point of inviting us," said Lucretia. "For the place is so delightful that we shan't need much persuading."

"You are all forgetting the best bit in your praises of the garden," said Corinna. "You haven't mentioned that among its other charms there's the very important fact that there are no men here."

"And *you*'ve forgotten an important thing, too," Helena added, "that the lady of the house is so kind and charming that that alone would be enough to make us wish to come back often."

"That's true," said Adriana. "Charming, sweet, lovely—no one could deny it. But it's a pity that you don't think of remarrying, Leonora, young and lovely as you are."

"Remarrying, eh?" replied Leonora. "I'd rather drown than submit again to a man! I have just escaped from servitude and suffering and you're asking me to go back again of my own free will and get tangled up in all that again? God preserve me!"

And all the others agreed that she was talking sense and that she was fortunate to be in the position she was. And Cornelia, kissing her, said, "Bless you, my sister! You're a wiser woman than I knew."

"Come, that's enough of all that," said Leonora. "Will you not all take some refreshment while the wine is cool?"

And so they went and ate some fruit and diverted themselves for a while, safe in the knowledge that there was no one there to see them or overhear them. When they had finished eating, Cornelia asked Leonora whether she knew what the figures around the fountain represented and, if so, whether she would be kind enough to explain it to them.

"I shall, with pleasure," Leonora replied. "First, I must remind you that this house, together with this garden, belonged to an aunt of mine: you must have heard about her, though I know none of you can have met her, as she lived in Padua for many years (she has just passed away there, in fact). This aunt, from the time she was a girl, was resolved never to marry and so, on the good income she inherited from my grandfather, she transformed this garden into the beautiful state in which you see it now; and at the same time she had this fountain built, with these figures, as a statement of the way in which she intended to live her life and of the views she held against the male sex. For the first figure is there to represent Chastity, to which she was devoted; and the meaning of the device and the motto are clear enough in themselves. The next figure represents Solitude and her device is the phoenix, to show that my aunt enjoyed living alone and that she lived on her own terms and, after death, was reborn in the fame she gained by her good works. The third is Liberty and her device is the sun, which stands free and alone, giving light to itself and sharing its light with the whole universe, to show that my aunt, living free and alone as she did, won a shining renown through her many fine and respected qualities; and also that she shared the treasures of her mind with every person of refinement with whom she came into contact—something she might not have been able to do under the rule and command of a husband. The fourth figure is Naïveté and her device is the butterfly burning in the flame, signifying that women (poor wretches!), when they are to be married, put too much faith in the false endearments and empty praises of men, who seem so kind and charming that women allow themselves to be caught in their snares and fall into the fire that burns and devours them. The fifth is Falsehood and her device is a peach, which is shaped like a heart and has a leaf shaped like a tongue; and the motto tells of the deceit and falsity of men, whose words to women all speak of love and good faith, but whose hearts tell a very different story. The sixth is Cruelty; and the device of a crocodile means that men harrow and kill those women who become involved with them and then feign a brutish compassion for their victims."

"Excellent," replied Corinna. "We are very grateful to you for having explained these riddles to us and I feel much beholden to the memory of this lady who knew so much about the world and whose opinions are so close to my own. Lord! Why can she not still be here with us today?"

"One thing I can tell you," Leonora added, "is that she brought me up to share in her opinion. In fact, she did not wish me to marry, but my father insisted on it against the wishes of both of us; and now that it has pleased God to liberate me, you may be sure that I am just as she was."

As they were talking away like this, Adriana said to her companions, "Now that we have had this explained to us, what do we wish to do next? For the days are long at the moment and the sun is still very high, so that it's quite impossible to walk in the garden. So I would think it wise for us to retire into the shade of these cypresses and settle down here and amuse ourselves in whichever way takes the fancy of each of us, some making music, some playing games, some reading."

"That's a good idea," said Cornelia. "But would it not be better for us to choose some game in which we could participate as a group?"

"Rather than play a game," said Helena, 'it would be more fun if we were to tell each other stories or to have a discussion on some subject that interests us.'

And as all the women started disagreeing among themselves, with one suggesting one topic for discussion, another a different one, Corinna stepped in and said, "Come now, let us please elect one amongst us to take command of the others—and let the others obey her, for, in truth, in the private as well as the public sphere, obedience is not merely useful but one of the most necessary virtues. And, that way, we shall harmonize the desires of all."

Corinna's plan met with the other women's approval and by common accord they elected Adriana as their queen, knowing her to be a woman of great discernment and someone who, though no longer young (for she was past fifty), was nonetheless very humorous and of an easy and cheerful nature. So they elected Adriana and swore obedience to her for as long as their gathering lasted, and she accepted the charge graciously, saying, "As the oldest of the group, this role you have given me sits well on my shoulders, but, by other criteria, there are others of you who are far more deserving of the honor. However, since this has been your courteous wish, I thank you for it and gratefully accept the governance and command you have assigned to me, and I promise to maintain justice and to govern you in the manner that faithful subjects deserve."

And, after a while, having seated them all around the beautiful fountain on some boxwood seats provided for that purpose, she added, "I had been thinking, since none of us likes to be idle and since evening is still far away, that to pass the time we should tell stories on various themes that I would set for you. But now I have changed my mind and decided, since you have been doing nothing all day but talking about men and complaining about them, that our conversation this afternoon should be on that very same subject. So I hereby give Leonora the task of speaking as much evil of them as she can, and Corinna and Cornelia can join in and take her side. And since I have the impression that Helena is so captivated by the charms of her new husband that she has some leanings toward the male camp, I give her leave to speak in defense of men, if she so wishes, and she may have Virginia and Lucretia as her companions."

When the women heard the Queen's commandment, they were delighted at the idea of talking on this subject; and Leonora said, "Your Highness has given us a most onerous task, which would need stronger shoulders than ours; nonetheless, to obey you, I am ready to plunge into this vast shoreless and bottomless ocean. But I cannot believe that these ladies will be prepared to take on a case in which they know right is not on their side."

"If right is not on our side," replied Helena, "then at least propriety is; and you well know that many disputes are won not so much because of the justice of one side's claims, but because it has decency on its side."

"If that's going to be the whole foundation of your argument, that men have decency on their side," said Cornelia, laughing, "then you might as well give yourselves up for beaten before you even start. You would as well look for blood in a corpse as for the least shred of decency in a man."

"Oh, and that's the least of their faults," said Leonora. "But I am amazed that our respected young bride here, just because she has taken up with one man, should want to defend the whole crew of them and should immediately bring up this matter of their 'decency.' Especially since I'm not sure that her husband has behaved so decently toward her: in fact, I suspect that he has caused her to lose something she had before."

Helena smiled at this and blushed and said, "It cannot be said with any reason that it is indecent for a woman to unite herself physically with her husband, since in that act of generation necessity is the natural mother and license the legitimate daughter. And as you know all things that are licit may also be considered decent. So if the effect—the act of propagation—is not merely decent in itself, but legal and necessary, it can well be said that when a man unites with his wife, he is the agent and cause of a decent act, and hence a decent subject. And for this reason he cannot be said to have taken away any part of the woman's natural decency."

"Where that particular point is concerned," Cornelia replied, "you have made out a very good case. But you are starting to praise men too much, which is against the laws laid down by our Queen; and so I warn you that you will lose the dispute not just because justice and decency are against you, but also because you are disregarding the rules."

"In any case," said Corinna, "Helena has not managed to prove anything except that men do have some merits when they are married—which is to say, when they are united with a wife. Now *that* I don't deny, but without help from their wives, men are just like unlit lamps: in themselves, they are no good for anything, but, when lit, they can be handy to have around the house. In other words, if a man has some virtues, it is because he has picked them up from the woman he lives with, whether mother, nurse, sister, or wife—for over time, inevitably, some of her good qualities will rub off on him. Indeed, quite apart from the good examples women provide for them, all men's finest and most virtuous achievements derive from their love for women, because, feeling themselves unworthy of their lady's grace, they try by any means they can to make themselves pleasing to her in some way. That men study at all, that they cultivate the virtues, that they groom themselves and become well-bred men of the world—in short, that they finish up equipped with countless pleasing qualities—is all due to women."

"If it is true what you say," said Virginia at this point, "and if men are as imperfect as you say they are, then why are they our superiors on every count?"

To which Corinna replied, "This pre-eminence is something

they have unjustly arrogated to themselves. And when it's said that women must be subject to men, the phrase should be understood in the same sense as when we say that we are subject to natural disasters, diseases, and all the other accidents of this life: it's not a case of being subject in the sense of obeying, but rather of suffering an imposition; not a case of serving them fearfully, but rather of tolerating them in a spirit of Christian charity, since they have been given to us by God as a spiritual trial. But they take the phrase in the contrary sense and set themselves up as tyrants over us, arrogantly usurping that dominion over women that they claim is their right, but which is more properly ours. For don't we see that men's rightful task is to go out to work and wear themselves out trying to accumulate wealth, as though they were our factors or stewards, so that we can remain at home like the lady of the house directing their work and enjoying the profit of their labors? That, if you like, is the reason why men are naturally stronger and more robust than us—they need to be, so they can put up with the hard labor they must endure in our service."

"So you're saying that all men's hard labor," said Lucretia, "and all the endless exertions they undergo for us deserve so little gratitude from us that all they merit is the contempt you're expressing! And yet you know full well that men were created before us and that we stand in need of their help: you yourself confess it."

"Men *were* created before women," Corinna replied. "But that doesn't prove their superiority—rather, it proves ours, for they were born out of the lifeless earth in order that we could then be born out of living flesh. And what's so important about this priority in creation, anyway? When we are building, we lay foundations on the ground first, things of no intrinsic merit or beauty, before subsequently raising up sumptuous buildings and ornate palaces. Lowly seeds are nourished in the earth, and then later the ravishing blooms appear; lovely roses blossom forth and scented narcissi. And besides, as everyone knows, the first man, Adam, was created in the Damascene fields, while God chose to create woman within the Earthly Paradise, as a tribute to her greater nobility. In short, we were created as men's helpmates, their companions, their joy, and their crowning glory, but men, though they know full well how much women are worth and how great the benefits we bring them, nonetheless seek to destroy us out of envy for our merits. It's just like the crow, when it produces white nestlings: it is so stricken by envy, knowing how black it is itself, that it kills its own offspring out of pique."

"Not content to charge men with pride, you must label them envious as well," said Helena. "And you full well know that envy reigns only in inferiors, so you are trying to imply that men are inferior. But since it is envy that poisons the tongue of slanderers, if we speak ill of men, we shall be taken to be envious of them and, by implication, their inferiors."

"We are not speaking ill of them out of envy," Leonora said, "but out of respect for the truth. For if a man steals, he must be called a thief. If men usurp our rights, should we not complain and declare that they have wronged us? For if we are their inferiors in status, but not in worth, this is an abuse that has been introduced into the world and that men have then, over time, gradually translated into law and custom; and it has become so entrenched that they claim (and even actually believe) that the status they have gained through their bullying is theirs by right. And we women, who, among our other good qualities, are eminently mild, peaceable, and benign by nature, are prepared to put up even with an offense of this magnitude for the sake of a peaceful life. And we would suffer it still more willingly if they would just be reasonable and allow things to be equal and there to be some parity; if they did not insist on exerting such absolute control over us and in such an arrogant manner, treating us like slaves who cannot take a step without asking their permission or say a word without their jumping down our throats. Does this seem a matter of such little interest to us that we should be quiet and let things pass in silence?"

"But perhaps they do all this through ignorance," Virginia said, "and not because they wish us any ill."

"Now you really sound like the naïve little creature you are," Cornelia replied. "Ignorance does not excuse a sin and, besides, their ignorance is a willful vice and they are all too aware of the evil they are doing. In fact they accuse *us* of ignorance and senselessness and uselessness. And they are right about one thing: we are indeed senseless to suffer so many cruel deeds from them and not to flee their constant, tacit persecution of us and their hatred of us as we would a raging fire. But we should not think that they behave like this only toward our sex, for even among themselves they deceive one another, rob one another, destroy one another. Just think of all the assassinations, usurpations, perjuries, the blasphemy, gaming, gluttony, and other such vicious deeds they commit all the time! And if they have so few scruples about committing these kind of excesses, think of what they are like where more minor vices are concerned: just give a thought to their ingratitude, faithlessness, falsity, cruelty, arrogance, lust, and dishonesty!

"So, if, as I have shown, even amongst themselves they cannot show any mercy but rather despise one other and seek to harm one another, just consider how they will behave toward us. As fathers, as brothers, as sons or husbands or lovers or whatever other relationship they have to us, they all abuse us, humiliate us, and do all they can to harm and annihilate us. For how many fathers are there who never provide for their daughters while they are alive and, when they die, leave everything or the majority to their sons, depriving their daughters of their rightful inheritance, just as though they were the daughters of some neighbor? And then the poor creatures have no choice but to fall into perdition, while their brothers remain rich in material goods and equally rich in shame."

"You have not mentioned all those," said Leonora, "whose cruelty toward their daughters has been such that they have wretchedly deprived them of their honor or their life."

"That is something I can't agree with," said Helena, "and I don't want to hear you trying to make too much capital out of it. For *my* father has shown me every regard and, in a spirit of true paternal love, has seen to it that I was married, and married extremely well. But you have no father yourself and that is the reason why you are taking such a desperate line."

"Gently now," replied Cornelia. "Do not interrupt her, please, because one swallow does not make a summer. Besides, what you say does not surprise me. What surprises me is rather that men do not all behave as well as your father did, when we consider that irrational beasts, from whom less charity may be expected, work hard to care for their young, and the pelican in particular is prepared to suck its own blood from its breast to nourish its offspring, motivated purely by paternal love. For every wise and loving father should see to it in good time that his daughters are settled; and if by some accident he should happen to die before he is able to do so, he should at least ensure that his affairs are in order, so that the poor creatures, seeing themselves disinherited in this way, are not left cursing their father's souls after his death. Besides which they are forced, if they want to provide for themselves, to have recourse to those means that are blameworthy and despicable.

"Then there are others who are lucky enough to be left a dowry by their father, or to receive a share in his estate along with their brothers if he dies intestate, but who then find themselves imprisoned in the home like slaves by their brothers, who deprive them of their rights and seize their portion for themselves, in defiance of all justice, without ever attempting to find them a match. And so the poor things have no choice but to grow old at home under their brothers' rule, waiting on their nephews and nieces; and they spend the rest of their lives buried alive."

But Lucretia, who had been married by her brothers, could not suffer Cornelia to go on any longer and interjected almost angrily, "You are wrong, Cornelia—there are also loving brothers who treat their sisters better than they would their own daughters. And I can testify to that, since my father when he died left me very little and my dear brothers found me a husband using part of their own inheritance. And I believe there are many other such brothers in the world."

"Are you not aware," replied Cornelia, "that God on occasion performs miracles? Besides which many brothers marry off their sisters not out of affection, but just to enhance their standing and improve their own chances of getting a wife; but those who perform this good deed, even for their own interest, are very rare, though it is something all brothers should do. But now let us speak a little of sons."

"Oh, now what is there to say about them?" exclaimed Adriana, the Queen.

"What I have to say," replied Cornelia, "is this. How many wretched mothers there are who not only carry their sons for nine months in the womb at the cost of great suffering and give birth to them with great pain and danger, but also feed them, wean them and care for them with great love and equally great trouble and, if they have had the misfortune to lose their husbands, toil, sweat, and work their fingers to the bone to bring them up decently, in the hope of reaping that pleasure from them that one has from a job well done—only to find that, when these sons have reached the age when they should begin to support their mothers, they choose instead to reward their many labors and troubles by abandoning them and refusing to help them in their need. And, what is worse, if the mothers have money, these sons will squander it all, at the same time making their mothers suffer countless hardships, scorning their loving warnings and treating them with churlish contempt. There are even those who beat their mothers cruelly."

At that point, Adriana, the Queen, spoke almost with tears in her eyes, "Ah, but Cornelia, if you had had the son it pleased the Lord to give me and then to take from me, I am not sure whether you would speak in the same way. For he was an angel of goodness—nothing at all like his father, who was a cruel husband to me."

"This son of yours," Cornelia replied, "may have indeed been an angel of goodness, as you say, or else he simply happened to take after you more than his father. Or it could be that he was going to turn out worse than other men, for you do not know whether he would have changed character with the years. And it is all the more plausible that he should have been destined to change for the worse, if the Lord God took him from you early, so you did not have to witness this wretched spectacle. For I can tell you quite surely that having a wicked son is the worst misfortune a woman can suffer in this life. And the reason is this: that just as wounds hurt us more the more deeply they penetrate our flesh, so the son who goes to the bad, being flesh and blood with the mother, will afflict and torment her more than her father or husband could, because the bond goes deeper. And, since, in addition, love flows downward rather than upward, a mother in her tenderness will always suffer her son's evils, however wicked he may prove. That isn't the case where her husband is concerned: if she is unable to live with him because of the extent of his wickedness, after suffering long and hard, she can at least finally leave him, if circumstances permit. The same is true of fathers. But sons may cause far more grief and yet women will put up with their offenses, so great is the power of maternal love."

[Following further discussion of this topic] The Queen gestured to Cornelia that she should continue with the discussion; and Cornelia, remembering that the next topic to discuss was husbands, announced it with considerable relish: "Well, having spoken about fathers, brothers, and sons, it is high time we talked a little about the evils of husbands."

Almost the entire company was in full agreement with this plan, except for Helena and Virginia. "It seems to me," said Helena, "that you will not find very much to say on the subject."

"Oh, but what are you saying?" replied Leonora. "It's all too obvious that where marriage is concerned you haven't got past the opening words of the speech. You are just like someone drawing close to a fire on a winter evening: at first, you begin to warm up and the feeling is quite delicious, but then as you draw closer and stay longer, you start baking in the heat, or get covered with soot or blinded by the smoke."

"Let Cornelia speak," Corinna added. "She may speak ill of marriage, but it will be the truth."

"You have about as much experience of marriage as I do," said Virginia. "What do you know about it? Anyone who did not know you and listened to you talking in that way would think you had had a hundred husbands."

But at that point Cornelia, interrupting their argument, continued, "Women who are married—or martyred, more accurately—have endless sources of misery. First there are those husbands who keep their wives on so tight a leash that they almost object to the air itself coming near them; so that the poor things, thinking that by marrying they are winning for themselves a certain womanly freedom to enjoy some respectable pastimes, find themselves more constricted than ever before, shut up like animals within four walls and subjected to a hateful guardian rather than an affectionate husband. And it cannot be doubted that husbands such as these, through this kind of contemptuous treatment, cause the downfall of countless women who would be better behaved if their husbands were more kind and loving."

"You might add that there are some men," said Leonora, "who convince themselves that being so jealous and making life so unpleasant for their wives is the best way to keep them in line. Little do they know, poor fools, that their wives, seeing how little they are respected and how little faith their husbands have in them, finish up behaving as badly as they can! Whereas when a wife can see that her husband trusts her and is not going to interfere with her freedom, then she takes the yoke on her shoulders of her own free will and becomes jealous of herself. Because, quite apart from the respect she gains through her behavior, when a wife is treated so well by her husband, it would never occur to her to repay him so badly for his kindness, however many opportunities came her way; she would prefer to abstain and suffer and conquer temptations. And truly there is no better guardian of a woman's honor than her own will and resolve."

"I have a fear that my own husband may turn out to be one of these jealous and brooding types," said Helena, "for he is already showing signs of it."

"Just pray to God," Cornelia retorted, "that he turns out to have no worse vice than this! Think of all those men who have wives as young and beautiful as angels and who, even so, neglect them and make fools of themselves over some shameless woman (for inevitably you do find a few such amid the masses of virtuous women), who may even be getting on in years and have very little going for her. Such men inflict endless sufferings on their wives, even stripping them of their most treasured things to give them to prostitutes; besides which, they very often make mistresses of their servants and fill the house with bastards and expect their wives to keep quiet and bring them up for them; so that the poor wives see themselves turned from the mistress of a household into the prioresses of an orphanage."

"That's just what my first husband was like, my dear," the Queen interrupted. "I was young and regarded as one of the beauties of this city, but he showed no interest in me at all, and after two years he fell in love with a prostitute, who was quite old and none too salubrious a proposition, and my beauty and my caresses were of no avail and my patience no use in the face of his obsession. He seemed to hate his own home, our home; and all the time he should have been spending with me, he frittered away at the home of that corrupt courtesan of his."

"Perhaps she had cast some kind of spell on him, so that he couldn't help himself," Lucretia suggested.

"That won't wash," Cornelia replied. "Believe me, all that talk about magic spells is just words: men do what they do because they want to. And if you want proof, you will find men who are just as obsessed with gambling as they are with women. So you can see what the problem is: men have vicious tendencies, to which they give too free a rein, and that's the explanation for all the crazy things they do."

"It's quite true what you say," replied the Queen. "For it was just my luck as a wife that after a first husband who was so intent on running after other men's women that he didn't have any time for his own wife, I then married a second who was so taken up with gambling that I can't tell you what a wretched life he led me, until it finally pleased the Good Lord one fine day to take him off my hands."

"You've never said a truer word," Cornelia continued. "They get so wrapped up in that cursed game of theirs that they stay out all day and all night with their gambling companions and leave their poor wives at home, so that, instead of enjoying their nights in bed with their dear husbands, these women have to spend their time sitting by the fire, counting the hours passing, like the watchmen on guard at the Arsenal, and waiting until dawn for their reprobate husbands finally to come home. And when they do come home, if by some unlucky chance they have lost, it's the wives who have to suffer for it, because the scoundrels take out all their anger on them, poor wretches. That's quite apart from the fact that they squander all their wives' resources with this perverse and vicious habit.

"Then there are those husbands who spend all their time shouting at their wives and who, if they don't find everything done just as they like it, abuse the poor creatures or even beat them over the most trivial matters, and who are always picking fault with the way in which the household is run. And the poor women who are married to men like this gradually come to realize that they haven't, as they'd thought, left their childhood home to go and run their own household; instead, it's as though they'd been sent to a strict schoolmaster. In fact, the poor things are so cowed and angered by the fury and nagging of their overbearing husbands that rather than loving them and longing to spend time with them, they find them irksome and want them to spend as much time as possible out of the house. You can find endless examples of husbands who are irascible and intolerable in this way, though there may be different reasons why they are like that: some are bad by nature, while others undergo some kind of humiliation outside the home and then come home and try to give vent to their frustration by taking it out on their hapless wives."

"While we're on the subject," Lucretia said, "I can think of one example, at least, of a woman whose husband is so foultempered that she has no peace except when he leaves the house."

"That woman isn't you, by any chance, is she?" Corinna asked with a smile.

"Would that she were not!" replied Lucretia.

"Well, if it's not one thing, it's another," said Leonora. "*My* husband was one of those men who are so mean they're afraid to eat because it costs money."

"Oh yes!" Cornelia continued. "Misers are often regarded as good men, yet they too put their wives through agonies—they keep them short of money for food and clothing and, if their wives complain, they start putting the word around that the wives are ruining them and wasting their substance and have no idea how to run a household; so that the poor things find that without having taken a vow of poverty they have become nuns in all but habit, with respect to all the basic necessities they are lacking.

"Let's leave this complaining about husbands to one side for a moment," said Corinna, "and talk about the worse type of man there is: the false and deceitful lover."

"Now there you're really talking about a task that's not for lightweights," said the Queen. "Not because of the loftiness of the subject matter, of course: I'm talking about its sheer difficulty. In fact, I can't imagine you'll be able to cover the tiniest part of what there is to say on the subject, let alone to find a safe route across this mighty ocean. Still, plunge in happily, for on the way out, you can always ask Love to lend you his wings. If not, you will need the waxed wings of Daedalus to make your escape, before those countless lovers against whom you are preparing to speak all turn their wrath against you."

"I have nothing to say against true lovers (if any such exist)," replied Cornelia. "My targets are those who pass as lovers but who are actually quite the opposite."

"Oh, come now, Cornelia dearest," said Virginia. "Are you now going to try to claim that lovers are as flawed as you have shown all other conditions of men to be? If I saw before me a well-mannered young man, behaving respectfully, sensibly, and politely, not staring at me, not complaining, not asking for anything, but just showing with his burning sighs and other subtle signs that he loves me and will serve me faithfully and that, in short, he is mine and mine alone—I could never believe that such a man would ever deceive me. On the contrary, it would seem to me as though I could see his heart lying open before me and I should be overcome by his displays of love and humility and would not be able to help loving him in return."

"You have just painted the outward semblance of a lover, as

though his inner self must necessarily conform to this appearance," replied Cornelia. "You poor thing, it's very clear that you've had no experience in these things—and please God you may remain so innocent! Not that I'm speaking from experience myself, but surely you too must have read or heard all those endless cautionary tales, which have enabled a woman like me to learn all too well, at others' expense, what this love business is all about? Believe me, lovers such as you described scarcely exist (ones that truly love, I mean, rather than just look the part). And it's these ingratiating striplings of yours who are to be avoided most of all, for, being young and thus more fiery in their passions than older men, they are also more impetuous and unstable in their affections. They are also foolish, even though they think they know better than anyone else; besides which they are proud, insolent, and utterly shameless, so that even though they hardly know what the word 'love' means, they expect to be loved, obeyed, granted favors, and, in short, given everything they demand. And these young men go about everything so indiscreetly and openly that everyone knows about it. As soon as they are the least bit in love, they lose all patience; once they realize that they are loved, they lose all discretion; if they are given some favor, they want the whole world to know about it; if they deceive a woman, they boast about it, do her down in public and glory in their cunning; and, if they manage to possess a woman, they immediately lose interest in her. Their love is no more than a flash in the pan; their loyalty, a laugh in the tavern; their devotion, a day out hunting the hare; their fine appearance, a peacock's tail. The only good thing about these young boys, from a woman's point of view, is that being so fickle and changeable, as I have said, they cannot hide their falseness and treachery for long. They are like bronze with a layer of gilding: it takes very little for that thin layer to start peeling off, so any woman with half a brain becomes aware very quickly what they're up to and doesn't allow herself to be trapped so easily in their snares; she either casts them aside or uses these frivolous creatures as a pastime, to amuse herself—like a fan made of light plumes, whose only use is for cooling you down in the summer."

"Oh, you really have it in for these poor little lads," Helena said at this point. "What do you have to say about more mature lovers? Can't we trust older men, at least, when they appear to love faithfully?"

"We can trust them even less than those I've been talking about," Cornelia replied. "For their experience has taught them not to love more truly, but rather to deceive more effectively. Dearest sister, the greatest threat to our innocence comes precisely from these more experienced lovers, fiendish creatures that they are! And you mustn't be taken in for a moment when you see them pining away in front of your eyes, consumed by their love for you, looking up at you with their piteous eyes and speaking honeyed words. Just think of them as an unreliable clock that tells you it's ten o'clock when it's in fact barely two. These men never really take a woman into their ungrateful hearts. When they meet a woman, they pretend to be her slave and to love her desperately, but at the same time they are laying down traps for every woman they see, trying out each one in turn, deceiving them all, saying the same words to each and laying down the same nets. These men, if nature has endowed them with some talent or charm or beauty or prowess, are so proud and vain that they behave as though women should be grateful to them for courting them. If they realize that these qualities of theirs have made a woman fall in love with them, they immediately demand a full satisfaction of all their desires, and, if they encounter any difficulty or resistance, they immediately get offended and pretend they want to claim back that heart which in reality they never gave away. Sensible women will regard this kind of lover as being like the panther, the cruelest of all animals, which, when it is hungry, pretends to be dead, so that other animals do not fear to come near it; and the poor incautious little things, attracted by the beauty of its spotted coat and lulled into a false sense of security by its cunning, are emboldened to come up and play around it; until finally it leaps on them and dispatches them ferociously and devours them, feeding ravenously on their flesh. The only advantage mature lovers have over younger men is that, being older and wanting to be thought wiser and better than they in fact are, they conduct things rather more discreetly than the others and handle things rather more shrewdly."

"My dear Cornelia," said Virginia. "What you're saying is sowing confusion throughout the whole kingdom of love. What of all the famous stories of lovers in the past? Haven't you read about all those countless men who have died for the great love they have borne for women?"

"Do you really believe," Cornelia replied, "that everything historians tell us about men—or about women—is actually true? You ought to consider the fact that these histories have been written by men, who never tell the truth except by accident. Even accepting that there have been many men who have gone wretchedly to their deaths while flaunting their love for a woman, do you believe that the real reason for their downfall is the overwhelming passion they feel? Not on your life! The cause of death is their overwhelming rage at not having enjoyed the victory they so longed for: that of deceiving and ruining these women whom they purported to love. As evidence of this, you'll find that very few men have died for love *after* achieving love's supreme end."

"Well, that's enough about these middle-aged lovers," said Virginia. "Are you saying that we should love old men, then, since we can't have youths, still less men in their prime?"

"That's not my point at all," replied Cornelia. "Old men are just as crafty as middle-aged men—worse, in fact; and, besides, they are deficient in many ways, because their years of happiness are long over and all their charm and beauty have faded: they've used up all the best of their flour and there's nothing left in them except chaff or bran. Besides which, they are extremely jealous and suspicious by nature, lazy and averse to the dangers, the ordeals, and the long vigils lovers have to suffer; and they are also fussy and mean. Though when I talk about their being mean, it's not because I think lovers should seek to buy their way into a lady's good graces, or that any woman should wish this of her lover. The reason I mention meanness is that when a man is mean with money, which is the last thing in the world we should care about, that's a sign that he must be just as mean with his heart. And that, after all, is the most precious jewel, the greatest treasure a lover can give to his lady and that she can give him in return; and that's the reason why true love is said to make people liberal and magnanimous, noble and brave. And, since old men are for the most part just the opposite of this, because of their age and all the ailments that go with it, let us leave them to one side. For they are more fitted to find their pleasure in drinking good wine than in chasing pretty girls."

"Now which men are you defining as old?" asked Virginia. "Up to what age do men deserve to be loved?"

"A man of forty-five or even fifty may deserve to be loved as long as he is decent and steadfast in character," replied Cornelia. "But I'll leave it to you to try to find such a man. For, young and old alike, not one of them truly loves from the heart."

"But tell me, pray," Virginia went on. "Those men who have labored so hard and spent so much time writing works in our praise—do you refuse to believe that they, at least, love our sex in general and the particular women who are the objects of their affection?"

"I'd say that they are no different from other men," Cornelia said. "None of these writers has been driven to write by the intensity of his love. The majority of them, believe me, have taken on the task of praising us more out of self-interest and concern for their own honor than out of any genuine concern for ours. Knowing that they have few merits of their own to win them fame and glory, they have used the achievements of our sex instead, clothing their fame in our virtues and perfections—just like those men who want to attend some ceremony even though they are not in favor with the Prince and have nothing decent to wear, and who take advantage of the invitation and the wardrobe of a friend and tag along with him to watch the festivities.

There are many, as well, who praise us in the belief that we are like that crow who let himself be tricked by the hungry fox, who saw the crow carrying off a great piece of cheese and started praising it extravagantly and, at the same time, begging it to sing a little, because it had heard so much about the crow's lovely voice; when the crow finally opened its beak to give the fox a song, it dropped the cheese and the fox snatched it up and ran off with it. In the same way, men think that if they praise a woman enough, she'll be so carried away by vanity as to allow herself to be tricked into releasing her grip on her own will, so that they can get their hands on it, along with her honor, her soul, and her life. And, anyway, what do you say about all those many men who have written attacks on our sex? Because for every one man who praises us, there are a thousand who attack us quite without motivation. So you should let none of these vain discourses persuade you that any man loves as he should, perfectly and sincerely."

"So we should love no one, since no man loves truly," said Virginia. "Is that what you're saying?"

"I don't mean to imply that there are no exceptions," replied Cornelia, "just as I acknowledged in the case of fathers, brothers, sons, and husbands. But what I do say is that those who love truly are so rare that they are lost among the vast hordes of false lovers; and it is extremely difficult to pick them out. It's just like those tokens you use playing the lottery: among all those thousands of blank cards you find maybe eight or ten winning cards, which only come up by an amazing stroke of luck."

"But surely," said Helena, "there must be some distinguishing feature that would let us identify these few good men? Some sign that would teach us how to avoid the deceits and treachery of those countless lying predators who stalk us to take away our freedom? And that would allow us to reward those few deserving lovers by returning their love?"

"Well, yes, my dear," said Cornelia. "But, as I've said, it's extremely difficult. If you were by some chance to find one who showed all the devotion Virginia was talking about, and who persisted in his love over time, without ever demanding anything from you that compromised your honor or your soul, then such a man would be a true lover and you could believe that he loved you from the depths of his heart. Another sign by which you can tell a man who is truly in love is that, if he happens to catch sight of the person he loves or hears her name unexpectedly, his heart turns over, his expression changes, his voice and whole body start trembling; he grows pale, sighs deeply, and speaks with a broken and troubled voice. The man who loves from the depths of his heart desires nothing, hopes for nothing, and demands nothing except to be loved in return; he keeps within the bounds of decency; stands in awe of the woman he loves; loves her in her presence; praises her in her absence; interests himself not only in her but in everything that concerns her, as though it were his own business."

[Following a discussion of the importance for women of being circumspect in matters of love, even if their nature prompts them to be trusting and warmhearted.] "Tell me, my dear, sweet Corinna," said Helena. "Why is it that women are more innocent and trusting than men?"

"In my view," Corinna replied, "the explanation for this lies in women's natural disposition and complexion, which is, as all learned men agree, cold and phlegmatic. This makes us calmer than men, weaker and more apprehensive by nature; more credulous and easily swayed, so that when some lovely prospect opens up before us, some enticing vista, we immediately drink in the image as though it were true. But despite all that, where our natural disposition is at fault, we should bring our intellect into play and use the torch of reason to light our way to recognizing these lovers' masks and protecting ourselves against them. In fact, we should give them about as much credence as the sensible little lamb gave to the wolf when it was imitating its mother's voice and begging it to open the gate."

"That makes good sense to me," said Helena. "For women's nature is such that ferocity cannot dominate in it, since choler and blood make up a relatively minor part of our constitution. And that makes us kinder and gentler than men and less prone to carry out our desires, while men, being of a hot and dry complexion, dominated by choler—all flame and fire—are more likely to go astray and can scarcely contain their tempestuous appetites. And that is the reason for the fierceness, waywardness, and fury of their anger, and the urgency and excessiveness of their burning, intemperate desires, carnal and otherwise. Isn't that the case?"

"Indeed," replied Corinna. "But men could certainly be good and emend their nature if they wished to, considering the perfection of their intellect, only they do not care to use their reason, nor to make the effort to contain their sensuality, and thus they go from bad to worse. So men are vicious both by nature and by will—and they try their best to corrupt us as well."

"Oh, come now!" Helena spoke up at this point. "Surely you're not trying to deny that women too have their part in sin, despite what you've been saying about men being the instigators and causes of all evil? That's nonsense. To take their part for a moment (for, after all, we are alone here and they can't hear us), what about all those shameless and corrupt women who dishonor our sex publicly, soliciting men openly and selling off their honor to the first bidder? Such women destroy men, stripping them of all their money and often bringing them to the point of death. And men certainly aren't going to let us forget they exist—especially since many of them are upright and virtuous, like Scipio, Xenocrates, Alexander, and the others we read about in history."

"Well that last point is true as far as it goes," replied Cornelia. "But you aren't going to find men like that often: they are like patterns of virtue that God sends into the world for others to imitate, and that's the reason why historians pick them out for special mention, as something remarkable, outlandish, and memorable, like those amazing comets that appear once in the course of many years. By contrast, there have been endless good and virtuous women. But where shameless women are concerned, the true cause of this terrible evil lies in the men who trapped, tempted, solicited, and lured on these women while they still had their honor, leading the most naïve and easygoing of them to fall head-over-heels to their ruin. But despite that, these women, wretched as they are, preserve a little more dignity than the men they consort with, because at least they aren't the ones paying the men; whereas men fall into their traps like animals and pay for *them*, however corrupt, vile, and wretched they are. Which is something that certainly wouldn't happen if they showed some of that modesty and virtue we find in women.

"Just tell me: have you ever come across the case of a young girl, a virgin, so bold and shameless as to tempt a man into vice? When a virgin loses her honor, it can be blamed entirely on some man who has shamelessly flattered and solicited her in all the ways he can find and who gradually strips her of all her natural feminine dignity and power until she is finally reduced to prostitution, either because he has abandoned her, or because some other hardship forces her into it. And once the wretched creatures are reduced to this state, knowing that men have been responsible for their downfall, they resolve never to love a man again, since they have been so deceived by them, but rather to give them a taste of their own medicine. And, just as men once preyed on their honor, they prey on men's purses; they pretend to love them and if, by some chance, a man falls in love with one of them (for it does happen sometimes that men get more involved with these women than with decent women, because these women have become like men and share their propensity to vice)—if that happens, I can tell you, that's the end of him, because they will drain him to the last penny, just as he deserves.

"And besides all this, those poor women have only one sin, whereas most men have endless vices. So why should so much blame be heaped on our sex? I'm not denying that it is a most shocking and shameful thing, but it is unfair that all women should be blamed for the transgressions of a few. Though even those few do not deserve to get all the blame while men stand by smugly congratulating themselves, because I have not come across any divine law that absolves men of this sin and punishes women alone. And even in human law, when the courts find themselves with a great number of culprits on their hands after some major crime, they generally try to establish who the ringleader was; and once they find him, they very often absolve his accomplices and punish only the principal mover in the crime. So you can see that both human and divine laws demand that wicked men should receive the same opprobrium and punishment as wicked women—indeed more, since they are the cause and the instigators of women's errors. And besides all this, those few women who fall into sin in this way (I am not talking about prostitutes any more) are led into it, as I have said, by their good nature and compassion."

"Oh come now, Cornelia dearest," said Lucretia. "You're not trying to tell us that vice is goodness? That really is a load of nonsense you're trying to make us swallow."

"But when you hear men talking," said Cornelia, "all they ever do is speak ill of women. 'Did you know what such-and-such a woman is up to with such-and-such a man?' 'And that other one! What a whore! What a slut! I'd never have believed it: she seemed like such a saint!' 'Oh, these women all make out that they're so prudish because they haven't got the opportunity. If they had, they'd all be at it; there'd be no stopping them.' And they can keep up these curses and insults all day without once looking down at themselves and seeing that they may need to take some of the blame. And I don't quite know how they've managed to make this law in their favor, or who exactly it was who gave them a greater license to sin than is allowed to us; and if the fault is common to both sexes (as they can hardly deny), why should the blame not be as well? What makes them think they can boast of the same thing that in women brings only shame?"

"Oh, let them get on with it!" said Corinna. "They think they have shamed and lowered us by introducing this convention into the world, but in fact it works to our advantage and their disadvantage, because it teaches us to avoid their company, which, in any case, is beneath us."

"Who knows?" said Leonora. "Perhaps it was women themselves—some wise and courageous women of ancient times—who first introduced this distinction between the ways in which men and women are treated. For when a man has amorous concourse with a woman, the result is the greatest shame for her and a certain amount of credit and praise for him; so that the woman always tries to disguise it as much as possible, while the man cannot wait to tell the whole world about it, as though his glory and happiness depended on it. Surely this is a way of declaring clearly the dignity and nobility of women and the corresponding indignity of men. Because, since this great gulf in perfection exists between the sexes, it is a very shameful thing when we stoop so far as to have anything to do with these inferior creatures—especially outside the necessity of marriage, which, since it is imposed on us, we can hardly avoid.

"But even in marriage, this intercourse with men abases us. For the ancient Romans held virgins in great esteem and treasured them and honored them as something sacred—as have all peoples, in fact; and the same thing applies in our own day, right across the world. The vestal Tuccia, who had never had intercourse with a man, was able to carry water in a sieve. Claudia, too, another vestal, was able to pull to the shore with her girdle the ship that so many thousand men had been unable to shift. For a woman, when she is segregated from male contact, has something divine about her and can achieve miracles. That certainly isn't the case with men, because it is only when a man has taken a wife that he is considered a real man and that he reaches the peak of happiness, honor, and greatness. The Romans in their day did not confer any important responsibilities on any man who did not have a wife; they did not allow him to take up a public office or to perform any serious duties relating to the republic.

"And if you want further proof of women's superior dignity and authority, just think about the fact that if a man is married to a wise, modest, and virtuous woman, even if he is the most ignorant, shameless, and corrupt creature who has ever lived, he will never, for all his wickedness, be able to tarnish his wife's reputation in the least. But if, through some mischance, a woman is lured by some persistent and unscrupulous admirer into losing her honor, then her husband is instantly and utterly shamed and dishonored by her act, however good, wise, and respectable he may be himself—as if he depended on her, rather than she on him. And, indeed, just as a pain in the head causes the whole body to languish, so when women (who are superior by nature and thus legitimately the head and superior of their husbands) suffer some affront, so their husbands, as appendages and dependents, are also subject to the same misfortune and come to share in the ills of their wives as well as in their good fortune."

"It's quite true," said Cornelia, "that if we were not by nature so kind, compassionate, and meek, then these facts alone would be enough to make us avoid men's company altogether, since it can bring us only harm, shame, and downright ruin. We should be more circumspect, and preserve our dignity and our natural feminine authority, without mixing so much with these creatures, who are not only unworthy of us, but also speak ill of us into the bargain, when it is they who are responsible for all our ills."

"Oh, but when all's said and done," said Lucretia, "with all these arguments of yours, you surely can't deny that women have been and still are the cause of countless evils in the world. That's the reason they are known as 'women,' in fact: the word *donna* derives from *danno*, or harm."

"That's not true!" replied Corinna. "Women are called *donne* to signify that they are a *dono celeste*, a gift or donation sent from heaven to bring goodness and beauty to the world. Why *danno*, for heaven's sake?"

At this point, Helena broke in: "So who was the cause of the Fall, if not Eve, the first woman?"

"On the contrary, the blame lies with Adam," replied Corinna. "For it was with a good end in mind—that of acquiring the knowledge of good and evil—that Eve allowed herself to be carried away and eat the forbidden fruit. But Adam was not moved by this desire for knowledge, but simply by greed: he ate it because he heard Eve say it tasted good, which was a worse motive and caused more displeasure. And that is the reason why God did not chase them from Paradise as soon as Eve sinned, but rather after Adam had disobeyed Him—in other words, he didn't respond to Eve's action, but Adam's prompted him to give both the punishment they deserved. And, besides, how about the woman chosen above all others to redeem that sin? God never created any man (a man who was simply a man, that is) who could match that woman who was entirely a woman. Just you try finding me a man in all the annals and chronicles of ancient times whose merits stretch to the thousandth part of the rare excellencies and divine qualities of our Lady, the Queen of Heaven. I don't think you're going to have much luck there!"

"I must say I don't really know how to reply to that," said Lucretia.

"Do you really believe," Leonora said, "that men do not recognize our worth? In fact, they are quite aware of it, and, even though envy makes them reluctant to confess this in words, they cannot help revealing in their behavior a part of what they feel in their hearts. For anyone can see that when a man meets a woman in the street, some hidden compulsion immediately urges him to pay homage to her and bow, humbling himself as her inferior. And similarly at church, or at banquets, women are always given the best places; and men behave with deference and respect toward women even of a much lower social status. And where love is concerned, what can I say? Which woman, however lowborn, is below men's notice? Is a man of the highest birth ashamed to consort with a peasant girl or a plebeian—with his own servant, even? It is because he senses that these women's natural superiority compensates for the low status Fortune has conferred on them. It's very different in the case of women: except in some completely exceptional freak cases, you never find a noblewoman falling in love with a man of low estate, and, moreover, it's rare even to find a woman loving someone (apart from her husband) of the same social status. And that's why everyone is so amazed when they hear of some transgression on the part of a woman: it's felt to be a strange and exceptional piece of news (I'm obviously excepting courtesans here), while in the case of men, no one takes any notice, because sin for them is such an everyday occurrence that is doesn't seem remarkable any more. In fact, men's corruption has reached such a point that when there is a man who is rather better than the others and does not share their bad habits, it is seen as a sign of unmanliness on his part and he is regarded as a fool. Indeed, many men would behave better if it were not for the pressure of custom, but, as things stand, they feel it would be shameful not to be as bad as or worse than their fellows."

"I remember reading," said Helena, "that in antiquity they used to punish women's transgressions extremely severely by law, while men went unpunished."

"Well, the reason is obvious," replied Corinna. "Men may be wicked but they aren't stupid, and since it was they who were making the laws and enforcing them, they were hardly going to rule that they should be punished and women go free. And anyway, they made that law knowing that they would only rarely have to enforce it, since so few women went astray, whereas if they had wanted to punish men in the same manner, they would have had to kill them all, or most of them."

"Oh, come now," said Lucretia. "Surely we've said everything there is to say about these poor men?"

"Oh, anyone who wanted to could easily carry on," said Cornelia. "In fact, you'd never get to the end of it: the volumes would pile up, you'd wear out all known languages, and need to live as long as Methuselah or Nestor. All we've done is to point to a tiny fraction of men's baseness and iniquity, but even so it's enough to make you wonder how women can bear to so much as look at them, let alone love them."

"What poor wretches men are," Cornelia exclaimed, "not to respect us as they should! We look after their households for them, their goods, their children, their lives—they're hopeless without us and incapable of getting anything right. Take away that small matter of their earning money and what use are they at all? What would they be like without women to look after them? I suppose they'd rely on servants to run their households—and steal their money and reduce them to misery, as so often happens."

"We are responsible for lightening men's burden of cares," said Leonora, "when we take charge of the management of their households. We do not do so in order to dominate our husbands, as many claim, but simply in order to give them a quieter life. And it's certainly true that a man can never really find true domestic contentment and harmony without the fond companionship of a woman, whether she be a wife or a mother or a sister; without someone to look after him, and to share all the good times and the bad times with him. So it cannot be said that women are a source of harm in the world: on the contrary, they bring great benefits to the world with their wisdom, their virtue, and their goodness.

"And besides all that (and besides their physical beauty and grace) women have other merits that should give them a claim on men's love. There's our fortitude, for one thing—fortitude of mind *and* body, for if women do not bear arms, that isn't because of any deficiency on their part; rather, the fault lies with the way they are brought up. Because it's quite clear that those who have been trained in military discipline have turned out to excel in valor and skill, aided by that peculiarly feminine talent of quick thinking, which has often led them to outshine men in the field. And, as proof, just think of Camilla, of Penthesilea, the inventor of battle-axes, of Hippolyta, Orithya, and all those other warlike women whose memory not even the history written by men has been able to suppress. And where letters are concerned—well, that's obvious: it was a woman, Carmenta, who first invented the alphabet, and poems are called *carmina* after her. And what shall I say of Sappho, who was counted among the sages of Athens? Or Corinna of Thebes, who outshone Pindar in eloquence? And if women should be loved for their courage and for famous deeds, think of Judith's remarkable deed, or Tomiris's revenge against Cyrus, or Cleopatra's undaunted soul. Or think of the women of Sparta, who, when their men went to war, used to lace on their shields with the words 'with them or on them,' meaning that they must return either victoriously alive or gloriously dead. And then there are the Roman women whose great love of their country and desire to free it from the Gauls led them freely to give up all their riches and ornaments and give them to the nation—an action which prompted the Senate to give them the right to ride in chariots. It was the men of Rome who started a war by carrying off the Sabine women and it was the women who then restored the peace. The past—and the present—hold countless other examples of magnanimity and patriotism among women: far too many to list them all now."

"You haven't mentioned those women in Sparta," said Cornelia, "who, when their husbands were in prison, obtained permission from the enemy to visit their men and then removed their feminine clothes and dressed their men in them, remaining in the prison themselves to be killed as a punishment while they sent their men out of danger."

"There are countless other examples of our love for our husbands," said Lucretia, "but it would be superfluous to tell you them."

"It's men who should be told them," said Leonora.

"Oh, they know them well enough," added Corinna. "They just pretend not to. And then, on the other side, think of how many husbands have treated their wives badly. It's such a common, everyday occurrence that it's unnecessary to recite examples of it. But enough of this—if women deserve to be loved for their chastity, then the case is quite clear, and there's no need for me to say any more than what has already been said about women's constancy. So I shan't go into the thousand examples of chaste women of antiquity, Christian and pagan. And if kindness and tenderness are enough to merit love, it is well known that women are incapable of hating anyone, however greatly they have offended them, and that a single good word is enough to make them forget all the abuses they have suffered.

"If I wanted to prove this more clearly, I would need the pen of an angel rather than a mere mortal, for the merits of women are infinite, and the blessings they bring to the other creatures of the world. And since women are a source of such honor and consolation, the Lord ensures that they are born in greater numbers than men; and for the same reason, when a daughter is born, there should be the most profound rejoicing across the whole family. But, on the contrary, when a father is told that his child is a girl, he is put out and dismayed, and gets angry with his wife. In fact, there are endless husbands who make their wives' lives a misery over this, as though the wives alone were responsible and they had nothing to do with it; and they want nothing to do with their daughters. What malice there is in all this! Men should be delighted at the birth of a daughter, who will grow up meek and quiet and look after them and their households with devotion and love, but instead they long for the birth of males, who, when they grow up, will squander their money and swagger around looking for trouble, in constant danger of getting killed or killing others and being sent into exile—sons who will gamble or marry some unsuitable woman, or who are so eager to be the head of the household and to be free to squander its resources at will that they long for their father's death and cannot wait to see him out from under their feet. These, in the main, are the delights, joys, and pleasures that result from male offspring, as we can see every day from experience. It's completely different with daughters, who give no trouble at all: all their fathers have to do is provide a dowry for them to buy themselves a husband, so they have every reason to be grateful to their daughters, even though in practice the opposite occurs."

[Following a corrupt passage in the text, where Leonora seems to talk about the extortionate amounts now demanded for dowries]
"Dowries are paid to husbands," Helena said, "because when a

man marries, he is shouldering a great burden; and men who are not rich could not maintain a household without the subsidy of a dowry."

"You've got it all wrong," Corinna retorted. "On the contrary, the woman when she marries has to take on the expense of children and other worries; she's more in need of acquiring money than giving it away. Because if she were alone, without a husband, she could live like a queen on her dowry. But when she takes a husband, especially if he's poor, what exactly does she gain from it, except that instead of being her own mistress and the mistress of her own money, she becomes a slave, and loses her liberty and her control over her own property, surrendering all she has to the man who has bought her, and putting everything in his hands—so that he can run through the lot in a week? That's what a good deal marriage is for women! They lose their property, lose themselves, and get nothing in return, except children to trouble them and the rule of a man, who orders them about at his will."

"If dowries didn't have to be given to men and men gave dowries to women instead, then marriage would be a little more tolerable," Corinna said. "Though men would still be getting the best out of the bargain, because for a very small outlay they would be getting a great return: the treasure of the sweet companionship and true love of a dear wife. And that should be a sufficient dowry for them, since they have so much more than we do, anyway."

"You're right," said the Queen. "Men are completely wrong when they refuse to recognize our great worth, given that ultimately a man without a woman is like a fly without a head. And while we're on the subject, I remember going to the houses of various male relatives and friends of mine, who were unmarried. You'd think you were going into a workhouse: they were so filthy and messy, with everything lying around all over the place, looking less like a gentleman's residence than a rag-and-bone man's shop."

"Just think," said Corinna, "if men could have heard what we've been saying about them, how many much worse things they'd say about us in return."

"They'd probably write some contemptuous book about women as a reply," said Lucretia.

"Oh, they wouldn't be doing anything they haven't already done a thousand times," said Corinna. "I can tell you, men haven't been sitting around waiting for us to attack them."

"Yes, we can hardly aspire to come up with anything as old and tired as those arguments they keep churning out against us, without a shred of truth in them," said Leonora.

"Oh, as to that," said Corinna, "let them go ahead and keep conjuring up these groundless chimeras and fantasies, which aren't worth the paper they're written on and which I'm certainly not going to bother reading."

"Oh come now!" said Lucretia. "If men are as bad as you've been insisting today, then why are we still inclined to love them? What is it that leads us to yield up our hearts to them and offer ourselves to them as willing slaves for life?"

Corinna was on the point of replying to this when the Queen stepped in, and said, "I can tell that you two are launching off on a debate that isn't going to be settled in a hurry. But since I can see that the sun is now leaving, I feel we should call it a day and not sit around here in the open air keeping company with the glowworms. And so, as your queen, I order you to postpone your debate until tomorrow, when Corinna must undertake to answer Lucretia's question and to cover all the ground we have not been able to cover today."

As the Queen spoke, she got to her feet and made as if to rouse the others, who had been so absorbed in the conversation as to be hardly aware that evening was upon them. There was some discussion about where they should meet the following day, but Leonora said, "What are you saying? We have started our conversation here, and it is here that we must finish it. Indeed, so that we can get off to an early start, I invite you, beg you, and *order* you (if I may) to come around for breakfast tomorrow morning. That way, we'll have more time for talking, and you'll have more time to make the most of my garden, which you've barely had a chance to enjoy today."

And she insisted so much that the others, overcome by her courtesy, all promised to return the following day. And then, after a brief wander in the shade and cool of the trees, they all took leave of one another and set off from Leonora's house.

"Wouldn't it be possible for us just to banish these men from our lives, and escape their carping and jeering once and for all? Couldn't we live without them? Couldn't we earn our own living and manage our affairs without help from them? Come on, let's wake up, and claim back our freedom, and the honor and dignity they have usurped from us for so long."

Second Day

THE FRESH, ROSY DAWN had already made her appearance at the windows of the East and the rest of the sky was white and blue, bathed in the purest of light: a sign to mortals of a clear and radiant day to come. So Adriana and her daughter, and the other women in their own houses, having risen and dressed in happy anticipation, and performed their usual devotions, all climbed into their gondolas and headed for Leonora's house, which they all reached at almost the same time. When Leonora had greeted them with her usual affectionate courtesy, the Queen said to her:

"So, Leonora, you must be impressed at how well we have kept yesterday's promise. We promised to come and have breakfast with you, but in fact we've arrived almost in time to join you in bed."

"If you had come earlier," said Leonora, "you would have interrupted a strange dream I was having this morning—just around dawn, in fact. I dreamed (perhaps because of our conversation yesterday evening) that I was fighting hand to hand with some of those dreadful men of yours, and that I was wreaking havoc on them and giving no quarter, hacking them to pieces and massacring so many that they were all put to flight. There was so much noise that I woke up, terrified, to find that it was already day—and then I realized that all this racket had been caused by a battle between my little cat and a troop of valiant mice, of which she had made mincemeat, so that my room, when I woke, was full of blood and corpses. So that explained my dream."

The other women laughed at this ridiculous story, and Virginia said, "It would have been better if we had stayed with you yesterday. I'm sure, if we had, you'd have had so little chance to sleep that you wouldn't have had the chance to perform all these amazing feats in your dream and show such prowess and valor against those poor men."

"It's certainly true that if we'd stayed here last night, there'd have been no need to carry on today," said Cornelia. "We'd have carried on chattering away, and we wouldn't have slept a wink, so we'd have finished today's conversation already overnight."

"Wouldn't we just!" said Leonora.

"Well, do you know why we've come over to invade you so early?" said the Queen. "We want to take advantage of the cool of the morning to wander around your garden for a while."

"Quite right," said Leonora. "You've chosen just the moment to enjoy it, because the sun is still not too strong. Let's go! We can pick some figs and plums, and the grapes are starting to ripen as well."

So she led them into the garden and left them to wander around and enjoy themselves there for as long as they wanted, while she devoted herself to organizing breakfast. And when she had everything set out and was sure that nothing was lacking, she summoned the noble company and they all merrily sat down at the table. After they had eaten their fill, laughing and joking, they went back into the lovely garden. They settled themselves, by order of the Queen, in the same place as the day before, though much earlier in the day, and Corinna started speaking.

"The question you put to me yesterday, Lucretia, was a very important one. But don't go thinking that I've spent the night preparing my response. I shouldn't want to lose sleep over such a trivial thing, especially since the question is so easily resolved. Your question was why it should be that, even though men are a thoroughly bad lot, many women—decent, sensible women—still love them very deeply.

"My reply is that there are three different causes at work here. We need to make a distinction first between the different manners in which women may love men. A first case is when their love is sensual in nature and they are enticed by that love into committing illicit acts. The root cause in cases like this is women's naïveté and their wish to satisfy the desires of the men they love: a weakness which is the only real defect of our sex. But even in the case of family affection or friendship, where sexual attraction is not involved, women may be fully aware of the evil nature of the men they love, without ceasing to cherish and care for them. And the cause in this case is women's overwhelming natural charity and goodness, which can be compared to that divine mercy which lavishes love and concern on all creatures, however much they may offend it and however little they return its love.

"Finally, apart from these natural causes, many women's love, whether sensual or affectionate, proceeds from the influence of the stars. Women can be quite conscious of men's unworthiness and ingratitude, and aware that they are throwing away their time and energies foolishly on them, and yet they still find themselves disposed to love, through the force of astral influence, which contributes more than any other factor toward the inception and the continuance of amorous passion. And even though it is said, quite correctly, that the heavens can influence but not compel us, it is not certain that we should place an absolute and unquestioning faith in this axiom where the case of love is concerned. Because, to tell the truth, we can't be sure about how things happen in this world; there's no certainty about it."

"But couldn't these celestial aspects and positions influence men to love us, just as you claim they incline us women to love them?" asked Virginia.

"They could indeed," replied Corinna, "if they found the raw material in men suitable to receive their imprint. Women, because of the innate goodness of their nature, are perfectly disposed to receive the imprint of true love. But men are both by nature and by will little inclined to love, and so they can be influenced only to a limited extent by the stars. The truth of this can be observed in friendships, as well as love, because women make friends with other women more easily than is the case with men, and their friendships are more lasting."

"It's certainly true what you're saying," said Lucretia, "that these celestial aspects exert great power over us, especially where friendships are concerned. I can think of countless occasions, in church or at a dance or a banquet, when I have caught sight of people (of either sex, it doesn't matter), who, even though they are completely unknown to me, and may not have any obvious charms, nonetheless exert such an attraction over me that I immediately want to strike up a friendship with them. And then, by contrast, there are people who have never done me any harm and who may be full of sterling qualities, but whom I take so strongly against at first sight that I can scarcely bear to look them in the face."

"True friendship, true affinity, is the cause of all good," said Corinna. "For it is friendship that keeps the world alive: friendship seals the marriages that preserve the individual in the species, while the friendship and bonding of the elements maintains health in our bodies and brings fine weather to the air, calm to the sea, and peace to the earth, so that cities can be built, kingdoms grow to greatness, and all creatures live in comfort. When a man is at peace with his neighbor, he can walk in safety, eat in safety, sleep in safety; and all that he does is done in a spirit of tranquillity and repose. For this reason, man should devote all his energies to living in peace, in order not to add new miseries of his own making to the existing miseries of life. He shouldn't take offense at every nothing, every trifling incident; rather, he should be prepared to put up with a few little inconveniences, overlooking others' imprudence, pitying their benighted lives and trying his utmost to avoid conflict and to live as harmoniously and as peaceably as possible. For whoever lives in peace is living in God, in a certain sense, since in paradise there is nothing but peace and charity; and God himself is peace and charity and paradise itself. But some people claim to have discovered certain natural agents that have the power to bring about peace and concord, and others that cause discord."

"Ah, discord!" exclaimed Cornelia. "The destroyer of everything! It is when men fall out of harmony with each other that wars begin."

"And then, alas!" said Corinna, "provinces and families are exterminated, states overthrown, and whole peoples consumed. Meanwhile, in the air, disharmonies of the elements produce thunder and lightning; at sea, they provoke storms; and, on earth, earthquakes."

"Oh!" Helena said. "Talking of earthquakes, you reminded me of the one last year. Did you others feel it?"

"Didn't we just!" said the others. "And what a fright it gave us!"

As they talked on about the subject, Helena asked, "Corinna, my dear, what is it, do you think, that causes earthquakes?"

"The wind," said Corinna, "when, instead of wandering through its natural element, the air, it gets trapped underground for some reason, and cannot find a way out. And since, by its nature, it cannot stay enclosed, it puts all its energy into trying to escape, and it is this force that shakes and agitates the earth so violently."

"It's fascinating to learn these secrets of nature," said Helena. "And the disturbances of the air and the sea: how do they come about? Perhaps you could tell us something about that?"

"Those are caused," replied Corinna, "by the different movements of the planets, especially of the sun and the moon."

"The sun, indeed, has a vast effect on this terrestrial globe of ours," said Leonora.

"The sun is an extraordinarily rapid-moving planet," said Corinna, "speedier than its constitution would seem to permit, if we are to believe the astrologers. Passing, month by month, through all the various signs of the Zodiac, it brings us now heat, now cold, now long days, now short, as it approaches our hemisphere or recedes from it, and, with its equinoxes, it measures out our weather and our hours of daylight. This planet reforms the year, tempers the weather, and renews the world; it clothes the world in green, infuses the life force into plants and stones, and stirs animals' natural instinct to the act of generation, which is necessary for their survival."

"The moon," said Cornelia, "as I have heard, is a body that receives light from the sun. Does that mean that all its effects can ultimately be attributed to the sun?"

"No indeed," Corinna replied. "For even though the moon receives its light from the sun, its extreme humidity makes it very different in its properties and effects. The moon is closer to us than any other planet and as it follows its natural course, of waxing and waning, fullness, renewal, and eclipse, it causes an infinite number of different effects. In the air, the moon causes sometimes lightning, thunder, cloud mists, winds, rain, and storms; sometimes serenity and mildness. At the same time, it also alters the sea as it waxes and wanes; and it causes violent storms and dangerous squalls, as its movement stirs and churns up the ebb and flow of the waters. And, what's more, with its great humidity, the moon is extremely harmful to our physical health, and, as it passes through its phases, it exerts a great influence for better or worse over the course of illnesses. This is why doctors observe the phases of the moon very closely, because one could almost say that the moon disturbs and churns up the human body in the same way that it does the sea."

"Truly," said the Queen, "it's a remarkable testimony to man's wisdom that we can know even about these things that are so far away."

"If there are animals who know about these things," said Lucretia, "then why should we be amazed that man, with his divine intellect, has come to learn them as well?"

"I've heard that business about animals too," Adriana replied. "Especially birds, of which there are many that appear to know about changes in the weather and indicate them to us by various signs."

"We can see this every day," Corinna continued, "from our own experience of the domestic fowl we keep—cocks, geese, and so on—which, when they sense a change in the air, beat their wings, fly around, and screech far more than usual. But it is crows and ravens, above all, that act as harbingers of future events, good or bad."

"Oh, come along now!" Leonora interjected. "Forgive me, but you are breaking all the rules here. We're supposed to be discussing what's wrong with men, and all you want to talk about is moons and clouds and birds and all that nonsense. Now, if you want an example of something unstable, why not talk about men? If you're interested in natural disharmonies—well, again, men will do fine. And if you're keen on talking about something that flies through the air, what need is there to look further than men's brains, which flit around exactly like birds, talking about this and that, with no direction at all. What's the point of all this astrology? This kind of talk and this kind of study have nothing to do with us."

"I have not studied any discipline," said Corinna, "and this least of any. But astrology is in truth a very distinguished discipline, worthy of the loftiest intellects, and there were many ancients who wrote on the subject. In our own times, as well, there are numerous experts who have written a great deal on the subject."

"Oh, that's splendid!" said Leonora. "That's all we need! After telling us about astrology, now you're planning to list all the astrologers you know, one by one. And then what? You'll get back on to the subject of birds and start listing each individual feather on their backs. Go on, I can't wait!"

"That's not such a bad idea," said Lucretia. "Go on, Corinna, carry on telling us about those birds you mentioned earlier: the ones that predict the weather and other things that are going to happen."

"The ancients," said Corinna, "used to read auguries of future events in the behavior of many kinds of bird, but as good Catholics, we should pay no attention to these kinds of superstition. How many fantastic things the poets have written about birds like the eagle, the peacock, the magpie, and the swallow!"

"Men like to compare us to magpies," said Helena, "because we are always chattering."

"And to which birds might we compare them?" asked Cornelia.

"To the crows we mentioned earlier," said Leonora. "Because when we see them, we know it means ill fortune for us."

"One really lovely bird," Lucretia said, "is the peacock. Or, at least, it would be lovely if it weren't for that shrieking noise it makes."

"The peacock is generally thought to be both the most beautiful of flying creatures and the vainest," said Corinna. "It loves displaying the glory of its many-eyed feathers, but then, looking down and seeing its ugly little feet, it folds up its great wheel of feathers in shame and starts shrieking in that strident way, because it realizes that the rest of its body is not as perfect as it would wish it to be. And that should serve us as a useful lesson, to encourage us to keep striving toward perfection and not to rest on our laurels, just because we have one good feature."

"One bird I find amazing is the swan," said Lucretia, "which they say sings as it dies."

"It sings," said Corinna, "because it predicts and foresees its death, which is caused by those three feathers that move into its brain as it ages. Certainly, it's a rare and lovely feature of this bird's behavior, and one we should imitate, since we have the intellectual capacity to foresee our deaths in a more rational way."

"And the phoenix?" said Helena. "Can it be true what we read about it, that there is only one of them, and that it renews its life in that way?"

"It may indeed be true," said Corinna, "even though it strikes us as so extraordinary. But, then, don't you think there may be many things in our own part of the world that seem quite normal to us because we see them all the time, but which must seem impossible and prodigious to people from elsewhere?"

"That's certainly true," said Cornelia. "But what does the phoenix feed on? It isn't a bird of prey, like the eagle; and it can't live on grain, because otherwise it would be seen around in the fields."

"I believe," said Corinna, "that it sups on celestial manna and the aromatic exhalations of those happy plants found in the sweet-smelling, shining Orient."

"What I like," said Virginia, "are those little songbirds we keep in cages—goldfinches, chaffinches, linnets, and so on. But best of all are nightingales, which sing so sweetly, and those amazing talking blackbirds."

"One thing I really enjoy, when I'm in the country," said Leonora, "is hunting these little birds you're talking about. I'm just not so keen on getting out of bed at dawn to do it."

"Oh, Virginia, do you remember that time when we went sparrow-hunting with your uncle?" asked Helena. "What fun we had!"

"How could I forget it?" said Virginia. "In fact, I can't wait for this autumn, to go and enjoy those country pursuits again, though it won't be the same without you there."

"What I'd really like to do, if I were a man," said Leonora, "is to ride out on a good horse with a falcon and bag some nice partridges and quails."

"Oh come on!" said Helena. "We can't do any of these things without men to help us; in fact, we wouldn't enjoy them without men."

"Oh yes!" said Cornelia. "If there's one thing they *are* good at, it's trapping, deceiving, ensnaring: that's their speciality, in fact. But it's not something we would know how to do, left to ourselves, so when we want to turn our hand to these pursuits, we need to learn from men and draw on their help, since they are so expert and skilled at them."

[Following a discussion of springs, rivers and the cities that lie on them, water and the other three elements, fire, air, and earth.]

"Since the earth is contained in a narrower space than all the other elements," said Cornelia, "it is remarkable that it has generated so many animals, and produced so many plants, and that it contains so many different materials."

"It is indeed," said Corinna. "If you consider all the different species of animals that live and breed on the earth, it seems miraculous that there can be so many, and it would be impossible to describe even a tiny fraction of them."

"I can believe it," said Cornelia. "And the number of animals in the wild must be far greater than the number of domestic ones."

"Without a doubt," said Corinna.

"Don't be so sure," said Leonora. "There are more animals in the home than you think, they just aren't recognized as such."

"Oh, do be quiet, for heaven's sake!" said the Queen.

"Ah, madam!" said Leonora. "How many lions are there, how many tigers, how many bears that we forget to include in the total? How many even more savage and terrifying creatures?"

"Let it go!" said the Queen. "I know very well what you're talking about. I pity men, when you're around!"

Helena broke in: "I've heard that the lion, for all its fierceness, fears the voice of the cockerel. Is that true?"

"Well, that's what the natural historians say," said Corinna. "It's also afraid of the sight of fire. But even so, the lion is known as the king of beasts, because of its strength and courage, even though there are larger beasts, like the elephant; crueler ones, like the tiger; and more ferocious ones, like the wild boar and so on."

"Are tigers and leopards the same thing?" asked Lucretia.

"No, madam," said Corinna. "But there are great similarities between them, both in their skin and in their cruelty and fleetness of foot."

"I'm so enjoying this conversation," said Lucretia, "that I'd be quite happy to forget about detailing men's deficiencies, if you others were in agreement. I'd rather listen to Corinna and learn something new than talk about men's flaws, which are something of which we are all only too aware."

"I'm not sure about that," said Corinna. "Women aren't as aware of men's failings as they should be, or else they'd know how to protect themselves from men better than they do. In fact, it's easier for us to understand the properties of irrational animals than to understand those false creatures who are close to us in nature, but quite different in their character and desires."

"Something I've been wanting to know for a long time," said Helena, "is the nature of the hidden enmity that exists between the wolf and the lamb, the lion and the sheep, the fox and the chickens, the cat and the mouse, and between other animals of the air and the water. What is the cause of this great discord between the animals, so that one is always chasing, the other fleeing from it?"

"The cause is not any enmity on the part of the stronger beast," said Corinna. 'It's just prompted by the natural instinct it has to feed on the other animal; and it doesn't pursue its prey or devour it out of any hatred it feels for it, but simply because one is the food that Nature has provided for the other. And, on the other side, the weaker beast—for example the sheep— doesn't flee from the lion because it hates it, but rather because it fears it, since it too knows, by a natural instinct, that the other animal is pursuing it with the aim of devouring it and using it for food."

"If only women too had this intuition and instinct to flee from their pursuers and from death," said Leonora, "we wouldn't see so many of them perishing or suffering as we do. But instead, poor trusting creatures, they deliver themselves into their predators' hands; and then, when they are caught, it's too late to have regrets."

"You're still at daggers drawn with men," said Virginia, who couldn't help laughing in spite of herself. Then she went on. "But couldn't we come up with some kind of remedy to improve them a little? If you have wine in the house that has gone off, if you mix in some good wine it very often improves it; if you have a ragged old dress, you can mend it so it passes as new; and unappetizing dishes can be improved by adding butter and spices."

"Dearest sister," said Leonora. "I wouldn't know where to start, to try to disguise the taste of these rotten men. They are like mature trees, that have laid down roots: they are incapable of change."

"But even with trees," said Corinna, "it's possible to change their nature by grafting them. But I'm not so sure about men: they never really change their ways—except from bad to worse."

"It would be more of a miracle if men improved," said Cornelia, "and started producing good effects from their bad nature, than the strangest freak of nature one could think of, like birds being born out of trees."

"That's truer than you think," said Corinna. "For, though the former is impossible, the latter does actually happen; we read that there's a land beyond Holland where there's a miraculous kind of plant that, instead of fruit, grows birds rather like ducks."

"I can't believe my ears," said the Queen. "That really is an incredible natural phenomenon. Perhaps it's true then what they say about the trees of the Hesperides, which grew golden apples."

"No, madam," said Corinna. "That really is just a legend."

"And how about those bushes that produce balsam," said Lucretia. "That's not made up, is it?"

"No, that's the sober truth," said Corinna. "They are found in Arabia Felix, where they also gather manna, which is a heavenly dew; and all kinds of aromatic plants grow in the same land, like cinnamon, aloes, spikenard, ginger, nutmeg, and all kinds of other spices, more or less hot according to their different properties, which are used all over the world and have countless different uses."

The Queen interjected at this point, "In how many different ways Divine Providence works to provide for our needs! God has even thought to place these powers in plants to aid us in our infirmities. How grateful we should be!"

"Another thing this proves," said Leonora, "is how little gratitude we owe to men, and what a disservice they do us. For all things were created for their benefit and ours, and in fact men themselves were created specifically to help us in life. And yet they do their job far worse than trees and other irrational creatures, which never fail in their duties."

"Let's see whether we can think of any herb or plant that might cure men's indisposition," Lucrezia said, "since we have spoken about the powers that reside in them."

"They say balsam cures all infirmities," said Cornelia.

"True balsam," said Corinna, "which is gathered from certain bushes in Arabia, using little ivory knives, is a divine liquor and extremely good for our whole body. Balsamic ointment applied to the living keeps the face looking fresh and young, while, applied to dead bodies, it acts as a preservative against putrefaction and decay. So all in all, it's the ideal remedy for everything—except the disease you're talking about."

"I've heard that rhubarb is very good against fevers, once the temperature has dropped," said Cornelia.

"Yes, it's good in cases of tertian fever, single and double," Corinna replied, "because it acts against choler. For it to work, you have to choose a full, heavy specimen (it's a root, and comes from India). When you break it open, there are separate veins inside, some red, others white; then, as you chew it, it loses its color and has a bitter taste. It's hot and dry to the second degree, like senna, and is very similar to the kind of rhubarb we use in cooking."

"Isn't senna good for melancholics?" asked Lucretia.

"It's good against melancholy, yes," replied Corinna, "and against dysfunctions of the liver. It's also effective against quartan fever, when mixed with colocynth. And colocynth is also good against hardening of the spleen (the marrow of the plant, that is, mixed with a solution of hart's tongue fern) or you can make it up into a decoction with vinegar as a cure for toothache or a poultice to use against worms. It's not to be used alone, though, as it's poisonous."

"In that case, it must resemble man," said Leonora, "who is noxious when alone, and needs women's company as his antidote."

"Nutmeg," added Corinna, "is very good in pregnancy, and effective as an aid to digestion for delicate stomachs, as are pepper, ginger, cinnamon, cardamom, and carnation seeds and other such spices, all of which are well suited to those of a cold complexion, but which those of a choleric or sanguine complexion should take only in moderation. Tamarind purges choler and purifies the blood. Scammony too helps draw choler from the veins, and is cordial, when mixed with red sandalwood."

"Oh Lord!" said Leonora. "You're no nearer to finding the medicine I was asking about. You can find all the remedies you like against bad blood and choler, but men's stomachs and blood can never be purged, as their hearts and minds are terminally sick. But if only it were at least possible for us to find some cure for our naïveté, and the compassion and love we bear for these sick companions of ours!"

"That's a remedy you won't find in Galen," said Corinna. "And none of the other authorities on the subject seems to have discovered it either—or, if they did, they certainly didn't record it. After all, it would hardly have been in their interests, for wolf doesn't eat wolf, and men know very well which side of their bread is buttered: if we stopped loving them, they'd be in a fine state!"

"You do find, though, in some books, all kinds of remedies against love," said Lucretia, "like the skin of a freshly killed sheep, or the dust where a mule has rolled. And they also talk about making the lover drink the blood of the person he loves and endless other things. But I think that's all nonsense: when love has really found its way into someone's heart, I don't believe that anything except death can really cauterize and cure it."

"While we're on the subject," said Corinna, "I've read that if a man carries a hyena's intestines around, on the left-hand side of his body, any woman he looks at will be mysteriously enflamed with love for him. Now let's forget about such nonsense! Goat's rue and sweet flag are both good cordial medicines, while licorice is incredibly effective against chest ailments, as are linen seeds. You can either apply them externally, rubbing them on with butter, or you can add them to food."

"Yes, but when it comes down to it," said the Queen, "I'm not sure I know of any better medicine for the chest and stomach than a nice sweet wine or a malmsey or muscat—what do you say to that, ladies?"

"Quite right," said the other women, laughing. "A drop of malmsey, taken without food, is very good for weak stomachs, especially in those of cold complexion."

"Normal wine is excellent too," said Corinna, "though only when taken in moderation and by people in good health. The whites and lighter reds, especially, are good (though whites can cause wind); heavier reds are harder to digest."

"There are those who say that herbs boiled in wine are very good for one," said Cornelia.

"Rosemary, in particular, is often boiled with wine," said Corinna. "It's the best of the lot, and it really is amazingly effective against all kinds of ailments."

"How about wine made from pomegranates?" said Lucretia. "Do you think that's any good?"

"Yes, it's good when you have the fever," said Corinna. "And, on the subject of acidic fruits, they are also good as an astringent—quinces, for example. They are useful for all kinds of things: they help in healing wounds, and quince oil is good as a cure for spitting blood and vomiting. It's also amazingly good for quenching thirst."

"I like fresh walnuts," said Cornelia, "but I always seem to get a headache when I eat them."

"Walnuts and hazelnuts do cause headaches," said Corinna, "and they're very hard to digest. But walnuts are a good antidote to toxins. They're similar to chestnuts, though they're colder in nature."

"The Lord be praised!" said Leonora. "We're on to chestnuts now! And how about going on to beans after that, and cherries? This is like counting sheep: we're never going to get to the end. I'm sure you're just doing it to make fun of me and provoke me into interrupting."

Helena and Virginia were laughing helplessly at Leonora's desperation, and the Queen said, with a grin, "Now do let Corinna carry on for just a little while, and tell us whether, by eating too many melons this summer, I'm storing myself up a nice quartan fever for the winter, for they do say that fever is brought about by humid and cold things."

"Well yes, I suppose they are cold and humid," said Corinna.

'But if you eat good ones, and in moderation, they aren't particularly harmful. And pumpkins, lemons, watermelons, and other such fruit are also cold; in fact, doctors call them 'cold-seed fruits.'"

"Heavens above!" said Leonora. "I can't believe what I'm hearing! I keep waiting for your good sense to reaffirm itself, but looking at the great leaps you've made today in the conversation, I can only laugh. You were meant to be keeping to the subject, but instead you've launched into this great rigmarole about animals, trees, plants, and medicines. Don't you realize that it's already past three o'clock and we still haven't started? What have the kind of things we've been talking about got to do with us, may I ask? Are we doctors, by any chance? Leave it up to them to talk about syrups and poultices and all that kind of thing. It's absurd for us to be talking about them."

"You're quite wrong," said Lucretia. "On the contrary, it's good for us to learn about these things, so we can look after ourselves, without needing help from men. In fact, it would be a good thing if there were women who knew about medicine, so men couldn't boast about their superiority in this field and we didn't have to be dependent on them."

"We've now talked all about the stars, the air, birds, rivers, fish, and all kinds of animals, plants, and herbs," Cornelia said, "and we still haven't found anything with the power to work a change in men's minds and make them respect us and love us as we deserve."

"If only men could be moved by force of words!" said Leonora. "If they could, I'd try my hand at a public oration in the demonstrative genre: I'd shower them with praise and lavish every term of affection I knew on them, if only I thought it would work."

"Oh, that would really be something to hear!" said Corinna. "Would you really dare stand up in front of all those censors, those know-alls, who do nothing but carp and jeer and mock? You could try all your best logical arguments, dialectical syllogisms, rhetorical colors, but it would all be to no avail. You could form fine concepts, clothe them in fine words, alter your voice, vary your style, draw on all the right figures of speech to construct arguments, prove laws, or recall examples, but you'd still have lost your case even before you started it, and even as you began your proem, you'd find your narration and epilogue already mapped out for you."

"Oh, I'm no coward," said Leonora. "If I thought it would be any use, I'd have no problem in putting my case."

"I have no doubt of that," said Cornelia. "But you're too fiery; you wouldn't try hard enough to win them over."

"What a lovely orator you'd make!" said Helena. "Go on, pretend we're the men you want to address and give us a taste of your speech: what would you say?"

"It would be better for you to speak in the deliberative genre, addressing men on behalf of all women, and persuading them to love and respect us," said Corinna.

"Go on, give them something to remember!" said Cornelia; and the other women crowded around, trying hard to hold back their laughter.

Leonora began, "Dearest and most cherished menfolk, so prudent are you and so warm in your affections, that I am confident that you will lend your ears to one who speaks on behalf of all women, on a subject that touches profoundly on the interests of all of us. And inasmuch as the cause I bring before you is the most just you will ever hear, and my arguments the most unimpeachable, I can have no doubt but that listening, as you surely will, not as interested parties but as the most impartial of judges, you will finally give sentence in our favor.

"The case is this: that you men have until now been so much our enemies as to have devoted yourselves to oppressing and abusing us with all the words and actions that lie in your power. And since we are entirely innocent and have done nothing to justify this enmity on your part, we now wish to move you to take pity on us, swayed by the force of our innocence and our merits, by the force of your obligation to us, and of the prayers and oblations we are about to offer to you, and of all our other arguments; and to treat us henceforth with a respect that corresponds to the great respect and love we bear you.

"For, to begin, you know full well that we were born with the same substance and qualities as you, and that we were given to you as companions in this life, not as slaves; and you are also quite aware that because of our humble and unselfish nature and because of the love we bear you, we serve you and follow you, and are respectful, obedient, patient, and utterly faithful, and devoted to you, accompanying you throughout life and even to the tomb. So, dearest, dearest men, what reason can you have for not loving us? Loving fathers, what possible cause can there be for your favoring your male over your female offspring? Are we not your flesh and blood? Why do our claims go unrecognized, both during your life and at your death? And you, cherished brothers, why are you so cruel to your sisters? Why do you fail to care for them? Why, pray, when you happily pay for and nourish brute animals in your household—dogs, cats, and birds—why are you so unwilling to do the same for us, when we were born from the same womb as you and are of the same flesh and blood?

"And you, beloved sons, why do you show such little regard to your mothers, who have suffered so much for you? You came from our wombs and drank our milk, your first nutriment, at our breasts, and we have spent so much effort in raising you, suffering endless labors and travails. Come, in the name of our blood, which is in you, and of the labors we so willingly endured in order to nurture you, teach you manners, guard you from every danger—in short, to make you the men you are today—can you not show us some compassion, some respect? Do not despise us, do not abandon us; consider that if you are now men, it is because we are women.

"And you, darling, darling husbands, pray do not hold your poor wives in contempt: you know full well that you are one flesh with us and that only death can sever you from our companionship. Why then do you abandon us? Why do you so often strip us of all our worldly goods? Why do you fail to cherish us as is your duty? Alas! Is not all our devoted service, all the love we bear you, not enough to bend you to make yourselves one flesh and one spirit with us, as you should be by rights? Hear our plea, dearest friends and inseparable companions, for you belong to us by all laws, both divine and human, just as we belong to you. Come, be good and loving companions, and show us an example: for if you love us, then we will love you; if you pay us the regard due to a wife, we will pay you that due to a husband—we will even regard you as our masters, not through obligation, but through love.

"We have made you judges of the case even though you are one of the parties; we have submitted ourselves entirely to your decision; now we beg and beseech you to listen to justice and pass sentence against yourselves. Though, in fact, this sentence will rather be in your favor. Pass it, o men, and you will find yourselves happier with every new day. Grant our requests, and you will remove any cause for further resentment on our part, so that we can live out that short space of life that the Lord has given us, loving one another and living together in peace, charity, and love."

Leonora's listeners enjoyed this speech of hers immensely and it was a long while before their laughter died down afterward. Then the Queen said, "Well, Leonora, you certainly go down very well presenting your case among us women, since we are all on your side anyway. But I'm not sure how much success you'd have persuading the men!"

"If men were a bit more as their forefathers were," said Leonora, "I might try to address a good, old-fashioned proem to them; and, if the vernacular didn't seem to be working, I'd use Latin. But I'd not sure it would be worth the effort: they'd just try to avoid listening to me, knowing I'd be speaking the truth."

"And besides," said Corinna, "your Latin grammar wouldn't coincide with theirs, for in men's Latin, the agreements are always wrong. With them, a relative never agrees with its antecedent, for, if yesterday, they smiled on you and had a good word for you, you can be sure that today they will be inconsistent with the past and will show themselves your enemy. They have the passive of the first verb, but not the active, which belongs to women alone, because we love and they are loved. Of the genders, they have the masculine and the indefinite; of the cases—well, the accusative is theirs, because they are always accusing us of something or other; the dative, because they sometimes give us a good hiding; and the ablative, because another of their habits is taking things away from us (like themselves, and everything we possess). Whereas we have the nominative, for always speaking their names with reverence; the genitive, for being all theirs, and the vocative, since we are always lovingly calling out to them."

"Now men aren't going to understand you if you carry on like that," said the Queen. "And, anyway, how do you expect them to love us if we're always speaking so badly of them?"

"Maybe we should just try keeping quiet for a while," said Helena, "and perhaps they'll change their tune."

"We've already done too much keeping quiet in the past," Leonora replied, "and the more we keep quiet, the worse they get. If a man needs to reclaim some money from a person who has refused to pay him and he keeps quiet about it, the unscrupulous debtor will never give him satisfaction, but if he complains in front of the judge, then he will get back what is his by right."

"But if it were the judge himself who was the debtor," said Cornelia, "then I'm not as sure as you seem to be that he would give the sentence in the plaintiff's favor."

"Well in that case he would be an unjust and cruel judge," said Corinna, "because a true judge should be dispassionate and shouldn't let himself be swayed by his own interests."

"I'm sure all kingdoms and republics draw up laws and appoint judges to ensure that the people are well governed," said Lucretia. "But nowhere does the justice system work better than in this glorious city of ours, whose venerable laws are worthy of being embraced and adopted by any realm on earth, just as the laws of that wisest of cities, Athens, were adopted by others in antiquity. And as for our senators, who sit in judgment, words cannot express their wisdom, justice, and compassion."

"Oh, quite so!" said the Queen. "But then, what can one say about the extraordinary goodness and civility of the Venetian nobility in general? The city can justly be proud of its ruling class, as also of its loyal and devoted populace."

"But, then, while we're on the subject," said Corinna, "what can one say about the divine merits of our most serene Prince, the Doge?"

"Oh!" exclaimed the Queen. "It would be impossible even to know where to begin."

"What a lovely sight it is," Virginia added, "when our Doge passes by on his way to some ceremony or other, accompanied by all the pomp and splendor of the foreign ambassadors and our wonderfully dignified senators and most noble secretaries."

"Indeed," said Corinna, "one feels one is seeing a collection of precious jewels, the greatest treasures of our country passing before one's eyes. For these are the men who govern Venice and sustain her; these are the men who, after God, are responsible for providing her with all her needs."

"This city has always had the good fortune to be governed most wisely," said Lucretia. "Now, for example, apart from having such a great man as doge, we also have a formidable crop of excellent magistrates, who look after those in their charge with remarkable and unwearying scrupulousness."

"Good Lord!" said Leonora. "I can't believe what I'm hearing! I despair of you! How can you let me down like this? Are you really quite determined to spend the entire day talking about anything rather than the subject at hand? What on earth do magistrates, law courts, and all this other nonsense have to do with us women? Are not all these official functions exercised by men, against our interests? Do they not make claims on us, whether we are obliged to them or not? Do they not act in their own interests and against ours? Do they not treat us as though we were aliens? Do they not usurp our property?"

"That's all too true, sadly," said Cornelia.

[After a passage on military affairs] "It's quite right," said the Queen, "that people should honor the lives and preserve the fame of heroes, for by doing so they encourage others to give up their lives for their country. But artillery and guns have been the ruin of the brave knights of our time, for they prevent them from displaying their valor and courage to the full, and no army, however strong, is capable of resisting them."

"At least in the past they could fight without having to worry about things like that," said Cornelia. "How splendid they must have looked, those knights one reads about, who carried off their victories through the courage of their heart and the might of their arm."

"If only those times were still with us!" said Leonora. "I'd like to see us women arming ourselves like those Amazons of old and going into battle against men. At any rate, it's generally believed that there are more women than men in the world, so our greater numbers would compensate for the disadvantage of our physical weakness, which results from our lack of military training."

"Well, I must say that *I* wouldn't be accompanying you on your campaign," said the Queen, "for I'm a peace-loving soul."

"It would be beneath our dignity," Corinna said, "for us to engage in battle with our natural inferiors. For the rest, the victory would certainly be ours, even if we are physically weaker, as right is on our side."

"Indeed it is," said Lucretia. "But tell me, Leonora darling, what emblem would you carry into battle?"

"I'd wear an image of a phoenix on my helmet."

"You'd like to imitate the great Marfisa [a female knight in Ludovico Ariosto's chivalric romance *Orlando furioso*], who wore a phoenix as her emblem," said Helena. "You know what that elegant poet said about her choice: 'Whether it was on account of her pride, to denote that she was unique in the world in her valor, or whether she wished to vaunt her chaste decision to live forever in the world without a spouse.'"

"And what colors would you wear?" asked Virginia. "What livery would you adopt?"

"I'd wear the white armor and white surcoat of the novice knight," said Leonora, "and I'd bear on my shield a golden yoke broken through the middle, signifying freedom."

"That shining whiteness," said Cornelia, "would be just the thing to symbolize our simplicity and purity, but it strikes me that green would be much better, to bring us hope of victory".

"Fine," said Leonora. "If only we really were in that position!

I'd be perfectly happy then to allow whatever colors you preferred."

"I think green mixed with yellow would be a more exact and appropriate expression of our state," said Corinna, "as it would convey how thin our chances are ever to win our way into the good graces of men. For they are so obstinate and so perverse in their feelings toward us that even if we were to succeed in conquering their persons by force, we could never win over their will by love."

"Rather, we'd be better off dressing in vermilion to signify our aim of vengeance," said Lucretia, "with an emblem showing the sun behind some clouds, but on the point of breaking out."

"No, no," said Helena. "Since the desire for revenge has no place in a magnanimous heart, such as we claim ours to be, we would do well to wear dark red, signifying our happiness not at the prospect of our hoped-for victory, but at the thought of winning men over entirely to our side."

"In my opinion," said Virginia, "it wouldn't be inappropriate for us to wear black arms decorated all over with white doves, to allude to the steadfastness with which we love these men of ours and the purity and sincerity of the love we bear them."

"All these various emblems and colors," said the Queen, "are like a language that doesn't use words, and that allows people to reveal the innermost reaches of their hearts in a delightful manner."

"There are many languages that communicate without using words," said Leonora, "but the language of sighs is, I think, the most eloquent of all."

"Say what you like," said Cornelia, "but in my opinion, the most persuasive of these languages is the language of the eyes, which can in all truth be said to speak and to reveal in their outward gaze the inner secrets of the heart."

"Yes, when they're telling the truth," said Corinna. "But the eyes very often deceive, as well, showing one emotion in place of another. Sighs, on the other hand, never lie, for, although one can pretend to sigh without meaning it, it's very easy to detect the falsehood."

"Fie!" said Leonora. "In men, everything is feigned: looks, sighs, colors, words, and deeds. You can never discover the truth of their souls or tell whether they are acting sincerely—except when they are perpetrating some particularly grave offense against women."

"What you say is quite true," said Corinna. "But I really can't see you ever allowing yourself to be deceived by a man again."

"Certainly not," she replied. "But I cannot rest easy, for I'd like to see all of you safe from men's wiles as well. But to keep to the subject of colors, how many men dress in pink or green to play the lover, when dull gray or black would be more appropriate, to express the fraud and practiced deceit lurking in their hearts!"

"In this city of ours," said the Queen, "men, after a certain age, tend not to wear colors as they do elsewhere, but always to dress in black. And you don't often see women, either, wearing colors outside the house, except before they are married."

"Yes," said Lucretia. "It's as though black conferred a certain air of reputation and dignity on the wearer, more than any other color."

"One thing that's certain," said Cornelia, "is that Venetian women dress in a more attractive manner than women elsewhere. Just consider whether it doesn't seem to you that there's something truly feminine about our dress: it has a grace and a delicacy that are peculiarly suited to women. Women from outside Venice, on the other hand, often look mannish rather than feminine."

"More than anything," said Helena, "the Venetian fashion for women to wear their hair blond seems to confer an air of femininity and refinement, even nobility. In fact, for a woman to have a fine head of blond hair is usually enough for her to be thought a fine-looking woman."

"Oh!" cried Cornelia. "If men could hear us talking about these things, how they'd mock us! As it is, they're always saying that it's the only thing we're interested in, preening ourselves and making ourselves beautiful."

"Oh, let them say what they want!" said Corinna. "It's not such an insult, anyway, for the refinement and neatness of our appearance is a sign of the nobility of our soul."

"That's all very well," said the Queen, "but how about those curls, those horns, that men are always carping about: what do you say to them? I can't say I'm particularly keen on that fashion."

"I'd say," said Corinna, "that that style too is something that should be not merely tolerated, but accepted and praised, just as much as any other feminine adornment. Because this is nothing more than a fashion, a custom, and a pastime of ours; and when it is done judiciously and with moderation, it sets the face off very charmingly. But, anyway, what on earth has it got to do with men, whether we dress our hair on one side rather than another? And what has it got to do with them if we do what we can to look beautiful, and do what we like with our hair? After all, women were created to adorn and bring gaiety to the world."

"There are certain women who don't look good with their hair dressed that way," said Lucretia. "But I don't think the style can be blamed for that: it's more a matter of those individuals' lack of judgment and the fact that they don't dress their hair in a manner that suits their faces. It's just the same with women who don't take any care to ensure that their clothes fit well and that everything's in place, so you'll see them with their dresses slipping off their backs and armlets that come down to their elbows and other such oversights, which make them look terribly untidy and slatternly."

"That's true," said Cornelia. "But not every woman can be perfect at everything, and women who make these mistakes must have their minds on other and higher things, so that even though they want to follow the fashions of other women and look good, they don't put enough work into it or give the matter enough thought. Besides which, often some blame should also fall on the men to whom these women are subject, who either don't care about whether their women look after themselves and dress smartly, or who actively discourage it."

"But then there are all those other women who throw away enormous amounts of time in preening themselves," said the Queen. "In fact, I remember, when I was young it was a consuming interest of mine, trying to look beautiful. Though I have the impression that nowadays women dress up more extravagantly than ever and there are all these striking new fashions."

"It's not unfitting for us women to express our natural inner refinement outwardly, in feminine dress and adornments," said Corinna. "Of course, men say that all this finery we wear betrays a corrupt heart underneath, and often endangers our virtue. But they're quite wrong. Women's dress could hardly endanger their virtue if men would only stop pestering them. And to prove it, just think how frequent it is to see women of low estate importuned by men and coming to grief, in spite of the fact that they dress plainly and without any form of adornment. It is far rarer to see gentlewomen suffering the same fate, in spite of all their finery, for they aren't dressing up for any vicious reason, but simply out of a spirit of gaiety and to follow the custom of the city."

"While we're on the subject," added Leonora, "men often refuse to allow their women to learn to read and write, on the pretext that learning is the downfall of many women. As though the pursuit of virtue (which is where learning leads) led straight to its contrary, vice! What they don't see is that what you just said about women dressing up can be said with even more justice about their acquiring an education. For it's obvious that an ignorant person is far more liable to fall into error than someone intelligent and well read; and we see from experience that far more unlettered women slide into vice than educated women who have exercised their minds. How many illiterate maidservants, how many peasant girls and plebeian women give in to their lovers without putting up much of a fight! And the reason is that they are more gullible than women like us, who have read our cautionary tales and learnt our moral lessons and developed a love for virtue."

"It really is something," said Cornelia at this point, "that men disapprove even of our doing things that are patently good. Wouldn't it be possible for us just to banish these men from our lives, and escape their carping and jeering once and for all? Couldn't we live without them? Couldn't we earn our own living and manage our affairs without help from them? Come on, let's wake up, and claim back our freedom, and the honor and dignity they have usurped from us for so long. Do you think that if we really put our minds to it, we would be lacking the courage to defend ourselves, the strength to fend for ourselves, or the talents to earn our own living? Let's take our courage into our hands and do it, and then we can leave it up to them to mend their ways as much as they can: we shan't really care what the outcome is, just as long as we are no longer subjugated to them. And then, having achieved equality, we'll be in a sufficiently strong position to mock them as they now mock us; and we'll have a thing or two to say about how they spend a thousand years combing and setting the few paltry hairs they have on their heads and their chins; and how they wear their cravats so long and drooping one minute that they can easily be taken for napkins or kerchiefs, and so tight around their necks the next that they make them look like so many puppets; or how they sometimes wear their breeches so tight with their long doublets that they look like frogs, and sometimes wear them so loose that they could easily jump around inside them. And what's more, many of them have now taken to wearing platform shoes almost as high as the ones they are always criticizing women for wearing. And there are endless more silly fashions and crazes of theirs—far too many to go into."

"You make me laugh," said Helena, "with all this talk about how men jeer at us for our concern with dress. That's not my impression. What they *would* find ridiculous, I'd think, is hearing us talk about some of the things we've been discussing today, which they think only men should talk about. As for clothes and beauty, they don't mind us being interested in them, because they see them as women's proper concern."

"Well, they shouldn't find anything to laugh at in our having discussed various different subjects either," Corinna said. "For one thing, we've talked about them just casually and in passing, not because we consider ourselves experts. And, for another, we have just as much right to speak about these subjects as they have, and if we were educated properly as girls, we'd outstrip men's performance in any science or art you care to name."

"Well, that's it!" said Virginia. "I heard so many fine things about men yesterday and today that I'm beginning to feel almost converted to the position of Leonora and her companions. They've made me inclined to think I'd prefer not to submit myself to any man, when I could be living in peace and liberty alone."

"Don't say that, daughter dear!" said the Queen. "Because I have no choice but to find a husband for you. But I do promise that when the time comes, I'll keep searching until I find a companion with whom you'll be able to live happily, for I shall strive to find someone noble, sensible, and virtuous, rather than someone rich, spoilt, and unreliable."

"Oh, but please, mother dearest!" said Virginia. "I'll be much happier staying with you. What if he turned out to be a proud and arrogant man: what would I do then?"

"You'd be as humble as you could in return," said the Queen. "Because, since we must needs be subject to them, the only thing to do is to flatter them and spoil them."

"Well, yes," said Leonora. "Most of them are so stubborn and determined to have their own way, there isn't much choice."

"But there are some men who are less proud than others," said the Queen, "and if women play their cards right, they can be brought around. And besides, if this husband we're talking about is noble, as I've said (I mean noble in his soul and his bearing, if not by birth), then there's nothing to worry about, because humility is the mark of true nobility."

"But what if he were stern and terrifying, what should I do then?" asked Virginia.

"You'd be patient and silent and long-suffering," said the Queen.

"It wouldn't be any use," said Leonora, "because men often attack us even when we haven't said a thing."

"But we've said that he's a sensible man," said the Queen, "so he will soon calm down and see reason—all the sooner if you don't stoke up the fires of his anger by answering him back."

"And what if he were jealous, how should I behave then?" her daughter asked.

"You wouldn't give him any occasion for jealousy," said the Queen. "And, since it wouldn't be your business to be attractive to anyone apart from him, if he didn't want you to dress up and adorn yourself, then you'd stop doing so; and if he didn't want you to leave the house, you'd stay in to please him. And by doing this, you'd win him over and gain his trust to such an extent that after a while he'd let you do just as you liked."

"A jealous man," said Leonora, "is never going to change."

"He will if you follow this method," replied the mother. "In any case, if he is a noble and a sensible man, as we've said he is, he is bound to change, for the sake of his honor, and because good sense dictates it."

"But if he didn't," said Virginia, "then what a miserable life I'd have!"

"If the thought of that life doesn't appeal to you," the Queen replied, "just imagine what will happen if I don't marry you off. You'll still have to stay within four walls all day and dress soberly, without any of the finery and fripperies you're allowed now, because that's what happens to young girls who don't want to get married. And, what's more, you'll be deprived of that companionship that could be the joy of your life."

"Well, I say it's better to be happy alone than unhappy with your companion," said Corinna.

"And I say," said Lucretia, "that even admitting that men are as flawed as we've been saying, with things the way they are in the world, it's still preferable to have their protection and company than to be without it. For we poor women are constantly being assailed and abused, and cheated of our money, our honor, our lives; so it seems better to have one man at least as a friend, to defend us from the others, than to live alone with every man against us. And if, by some chance, as sometimes happens, one's husband is a good man, then it's impossible to imagine how happy a woman's life can be, living with such a man in an inseparable companionship that lasts until death. And so, dearest girl, you shouldn't lose heart, for you have no way of knowing yet what kind of future God has prepared for you."

"If she could be sure to find a husband like the one you've just described," said Leonora, "I'd certainly advise her to take him. But there are so few good ones around that, to be on the safe side, I would urge her in the strongest possible terms to shun marriage like the plague."

"That's enough!" said the Queen. "I'm not going to settle on a husband for Virginia until I've managed to seek one out who is as good as I promised. It shouldn't be hard to tell who is suitable by looking at their behavior (for I'm going to research this very thoroughly)."

"That's a very sensible plan," said Lucretia. "The thing is not to lay too much stress on wealth and beauty in a marriage partner (and that goes for both men and women), for it's that kind of vain concern that is the downfall of many husbands and wives."

"It's certainly true," said Leonora, "that since men are rotten for the most part, women should do what our Queen says and put their energies into seeking out that quality in husbands which is hardest to find and yet ultimately the most important: goodness."

"Oh, stick to your ground if you must!" said Helena. "Go on, don't give an inch! If men knew what you were thinking when they saw you walking past in the street, I'd have to start fearing for your safety."

"On the contrary," replied Leonora, "men have good cause to honor me and take my part, for, when it comes down to it, nothing of what I've said has been intended to offend good men; rather, it's all been directed toward converting bad men—if only they'd listen. So they should be grateful to me, really, since

I haven't been speaking out of any hatred for men, but rather in a spirit of charity, and moved by the compassion I feel for the many suffering women I see around me. For many men see the world in a blinkered way, and are so firmly convinced by the unwarrantable fallacy that they are created women's superiors that they believe themselves fully justified in treating women as tyrannically and brutally as they like. But if they could be persuaded of their error, they might just change their ways. So I don't feel that men would have any cause to be offended by what I've said, even if I had spoken publicly in their presence."

"Oh, if only you had!" cried Cornelia. "Countless women would have had cause to be grateful to you, both for the useful warnings you'd have given them and for having done such a good job of persuading those men who fail to behave as they should toward women to mend their ways and become better."

"Talking away like this," said the Queen, "we have amused ourselves so delightfully that the time we had for speaking has run out before the subject was exhausted. So, in order not to stretch things out to infinity, since the day is drawing to a close, it seems appropriate for me to renounce my sovereignty to your good graces, thanking you for the obedience and loyalty you have shown me. And, to conclude, I'd just like to beg Leonora to change her mind about marriage, since she's still such a slip of a girl, and to try to seek out a worthy and charming companion for herself, with whom she can lead a long and happy life—if only to avoid the risk of giving occasion for malicious gossip and slander."

"Well, let's see Virginia married first," said Leonora, "since it's her first time. And, in the meantime, I'll think it over, and, who knows? Perhaps eventually I'll come around to accepting your counsel."

With that, the women arose from their seats, for the sun was on the point of setting, and, as they walked through the garden in the cool of the evening, Corinna and Virginia started singing a madrigal:

If the stars adorn the heavens,
So too women adorn the world,
With all that is lovely and pleasant in it.
And just as no mortal can live
Without a soul and a heart,
So men cannot get by without women,
For woman is man's heart, soul, and life.

When they had finished, the women all took leave of one another and went off to their respective homes.

Further Reading

A COMPLETE AND ANNOTATED English edition of *The Merits of Women* is available as *The Worth of Women* in the University of Chicago Press "The Other Voice in Early Modern Europe" series (first published in 1997). The same series includes an edition of Fonte's *Floridoro: A Chivalric Romance*, translated by Julia Kisacky and edited by Kisacky and Valeria Finucci (2006), along with numerous other works by Italian sixteenth-century women. Of special interest to readers of Fonte are the *Poems and Selected Letters* of the Venetian courtesan and writer Veronica Franco (translated and edited by Ann Rosalind Jones and Margaret Rosenthal, 1998); and two works by Venetian feminist theorists working in the wake of Fonte: Lucrezia Marinella's *The Nobility and Excellence of Women and the Vices and Defects of Men*, edited and translated by Anne Dunhill with an introduction by Letizia Panizza (2000); and Arcangela Tarabotti's *Paternal Tyranny*, edited and translated by Letizia Panizza (2004).

The only monograph on Moderata Fonte to date is Paola Malpezzi Price, *Women and Life in Sixteenth-Century Venice* (Madison, NJ: Fairleigh Dickinson University Press, 2003). A critical essay setting Fonte's text in its social and economic context is Virginia Cox, "The Single Self: Feminist Thought and the Marriage Market in Early Modern Venice," in *The Renaissance, Italy and Abroad*, ed. John Jeffries Martin (London: Routledge, 2003).

A good general survey of the position of women in this period is

Merry Weisner, *Women and Gender in Early Modern Europe*, 3rd edition (Cambridge: Cambridge University Press, 2008). For Venice, see Federica Ambrosini, "Towards a Social History of Women in Venice: From the Renaissance to the Enlightenment," in *Venice Reconsidered: The History and Civilization of an Italian City State*, ed. John Martin and Dennis Romano (Baltimore: Johns Hopkins University Press, 2000).

A concise overview of women's cultural engagement in Italy during the Renaissance may be found in Virginia Cox, *A Short History of the Italian Renaissance* (London: I. B. Tauris, 2015). On the tradition of women's writing in Italy more generally, see, by the same author, *Women's Writing in Italy, 1400–1650* (Baltimore: Johns Hopkins University Press, 2008) and *The Prodigious Muse: Women's Writing in Counter-Reformation Italy* (same publisher, 2011), the second of which contains discussions of all Fonte's works. On Fonte's place in the history of early feminist thought, see Sarah Gwyneth Ross, *The Birth of Feminism: Woman as Intellect in Renaissance Italy and England* (Cambridge, MA: Harvard University Press, 2009).

Biographical Notes

VIRGINIA COX IS PROFESSOR of Italian studies at New York University. She is the author of many translations and books on Italian literature and history, including *A Short History of the Italian Renaissance* (2015), *Lyric Poetry by Women of the Italian Renaissance* (2013), and *The Prodigious Muse: Women's Writing in Counter-Reformation* (2011), as well as *The Renaissance Dialogue: Literary Dialogue in its Social and Political Contexts, Castiglione to Galileo* (2008).

Dacia Maraini is an Italian novelist, playwright, and cultural critic. She has been awarded many of Italy's top honors and awards, including the Formentor Prize for her novel *L'età del malessere* (1963), the Premio Fregene for *Isolina* (1985), the Premio Campiello for *La lunga vita di Marianna Ucrìa* (1990), and the Premerio Strega for *Buio* (1999). In 2011 she was a finalist for the Man Booker International Prize. Her plays, novels, poetry, and essays have been widely translated; *The Train to Budapest* (2010) is her most recent book to appear in English.

Made in the USA
Las Vegas, NV
24 September 2021